Stadium Stories:
Ohio State Buckeyes

Stadium Stories™ Series

Stadium Stories:

Ohio State Buckeyes

Colorful Tales of the Scarlet and Gray

Jeff Rapp

The Globe Pequot Press

GUILFORD, CONNECTICUT

Text design: Casey Shain
Cover photos (clockwise from top left): Brockway Sports Photos, Jeff Brehm, Steve Helwagen/*Buckeye Sports Bulletin*, Jeff Brehm, courtesy The Ohio State University, and Brockway Sports Photos

Library of Congress Cataloging-in-Publication Data
Rapp, Jeffrey W.
  Stadium Stories : Ohio State Buckeyes / Jeffrey W. Rapp.–1st ed.
     p. cm.
   ISBN 0-7627-2731-4
   1. Ohio State Buckeyes (Football team) 2. Ohio State University–Football. I. Title.

GV958.O35R36 2003
796.332'63'0977157–dc21   2003056374

Manufactured in the United States of America
First Edition/First Printing

Contents

Acknowledgments

This book is dedicated to all those who supported my career over the years, especially my father, Wayne Rapp, a constant inspiration and the best writer I know. It's also the result of Ohio State players, coaches, and reporters past and present who were gracious enough to regale me with background information and provide me with an easy and entertaining topic. I also would like to thank the 2002 Ohio State football team and head coach Jim Tressel for their access during their stirring run to the national championship. Special thanks also go out to Archie Griffin, who somehow matches his greatness with his kindness.

Super Season of 1968: A Hard Act to Follow

J ust the mention of Ohio State football evokes so many memories, so many familiar faces, so many feats of greatness: Archie, Woody, Eddie; national championships; the Michigan rivalry; the Rose Bowl. But when it comes to the greatest team ever to grace the field in scarlet and gray all discussion has begun and ended for decades with the Buckeyes of 1968.

Life in America was a whir back then. There were hot-button political topics that ranged from civil rights to the escalating war in Vietnam. Key political figures were assassinated. Popular music, fashion, and values were undergoing radical change.

It was a tumultuous time for the Ohio State football program as well. The Buckeyes had never really been in contention for the Big Ten crown during the previous two seasons and fans were getting antsy for an expected return to the top. That anticipation was only fueled when Fred Taylor's basketball team, led by Bill Hosket, advanced all the way to the final four of the NCAA Tournament.

Could the football team take the proverbial ball and run with it? Only an eternal optimist could have foretold the magic that was in store.

The 6–3 season of 1967 included a 2–3 start and a glaring lowlight: a humiliating 41–6 home loss to mighty Purdue. The thirty-five-point setback stood as Woody Hayes's worst defeat in 276 games as OSU head coach. Rumblings were beginning to emanate from Columbus that Hayes's days were numbered—even after seventeen seasons and a pair of national championships.

Normally not one to fret about public sentiment, Hayes had no choice but to be a realist. He told his assistants that the only way they could insure their contracts would be renewed was to win the rest of the games on their schedule. The Buckeyes set out toward that goal by winning at Michigan State, surviving a 17–15 nail-biter with Wisconsin, and dumping Iowa. However, not many plunked down the $5.00 ticket price to see the Wisconsin game in a steady rain. The home crowd was announced at 65,470 on November 11, 1967, the smallest since the famous "Snow Bowl" of 1950.

There are still those close to the program who believe to this day that Hayes would have been fired if the Buckeyes hadn't won at Michigan.

But Hayes, as legend has it, was a fighter. He indeed led OSU to a win in Ann Arbor, 24–14, and despite the turmoil of the mid-1960s he went out and recruited a group that is still very much in the conversation of all-time great incoming classes.

This group included such budding stars as Doug Adams, Tim Anderson, John Brockington, Mark Debevc, Leo Hayden, Bruce Jankowski, Rex Kern, Ron Maciejowski, Mike Sensibaugh, Jim Stillwagon, Jack Tatum, Jan White, and Larry Zelina. All thirteen were drafted by the NFL and most were very productive players in that league, the fierce Tatum being the cream of the crop.

And it's not as if the cupboard was bare when the "Super Sophs," as they are still known, arrived on the scene. The Buckeyes returned a veteran offensive line featuring standout senior tackles David Foley and Rufus Mayes, fullback extraordinaire Jim Otis, reliable defensive linemen David Whitfield and Paul Schmidlin, rock-steady linebackers Mark Stier and Dirk Worden, and savvy defensive back Ted Provost.

Given the newfound pressure and the unique skills of his youngbloods, Hayes—who often said that "you lose one game for every sophomore you play" because of their inexperience—was actually telling reporters and alumni that he had the makings of a strong team with the youngsters filling in the cracks. The key to it all would be the play of the redheaded Kern, one of the headiest and gutsiest signal callers ever at Ohio State.

The Pieces Fall into Place

So, as the 1968 season approached, Hayes knew he was in for an unusual but promising fall. As freshmen who were ineligible to play in 1967, Kern and Company dazzled and sometimes frustrated the coaching staff with how often they showed up the veterans in practice.

"I felt we had a special team when Woody recruited us, but when we started practicing against the varsity I was awestruck," said Kern, a product of Lancaster, Ohio.

"They used to have us practice goal-line drills against the defense. Tiger Ellison was the freshman coach. He'd give us a play and say, 'It's fourth and goal at the 2.' Well, we'd line up, and I'd turn around and hand the ball to Brock and he'd score. Then they'd move the ball back to the 4 to try it again, and I'd just give the ball to Tate and he'd score.

"[Defensive coordinator] Lou McCullough would go berserk. He didn't know what to do, so he'd get on Tiger and say we weren't running the play right. We were; they just couldn't stop us. But Lou would have a fit and pick the ball up and put it on the 9, and we'd score again."

It soon was clear that the youngsters were already good enough to beat most Big Ten teams.

"We had so much talent Woody didn't know what to do with it," Kern said. "I mean, we had guys like Jack Tatum, who was probably our best running back, and he goes on to be the best college defensive back of all time."

For a while it looked as though Kern's debut amid all that talent might never happen. He dealt with a nagging hamstring injury as a freshman that dated to his high school basketball days. And in June of 1968, Kern underwent surgery for a herniated disk in his lower back. Hayes came to see him immediately after and told Kern's parents that Rex's education would be paid for no matter what.

> "When I idolized him as a youngster, I thought he did everything perfect."
>
> —Jim Tressel on Rex Kern

In just six weeks Rex managed to get through rehab and was named the starter for the September 28 opener with SMU. The game had fans buzzing. The Mustangs were a pass-happy bunch that featured star quarterback Chuck Hixson. The Buckeyes could only hope Kern didn't get caught up in the hoopla.

Hayes and SMU coach Hayden Fry, a sly fox if ever there were one, did not exchange game film. Fry tried to stun OSU by having his quarterbacks heave seventy-six passes, sixty-nine of them by Hixson. The total set an NCAA record for passing attempts by one team that stood for more than twenty years.

Hayes tried to counter that insanity with a severely conservative game plan, even punting on third down early in the game. With a few minutes left in the first half, Kern decided to try to change the complexion of the game. Faced with a fourth and 10 near midfield, Hayes sent Sensibaugh in to punt but Kern waved him off and called a play.

When Kern was named starter before the season, Hayes pulled him aside and told him, "When you're on the football field, you're in charge. There'll be times out there when you'll see things my coaching staff and I won't see and you'll have to go on a gut reaction."

This was not one of those times. Kern simply decided to be daring, and he understood the magnitude of what he was doing by breaking the huddle on fourth and long. "I'm sure there were people in the stands gasping, saying, 'Hey, this kid just blew Woody off,'" he said. "I think I shocked the whole stadium."

Silence fell over the crowd and Kern called what he now describes as "a terrible play," which sent only one receiver in a pattern. That player was promptly triple covered. The rest went after Kern. He was hit 7 yards behind the line of scrimmage by a cornerback, pirouetted away, hurdled another defender, and raced for 15 yards.

Moments later, Kern hit Dave Brungard for an 18-yard touchdown strike that put OSU up 26–7 at halftime. The Buckeyes cruised to a 35–14 win and OSU had its leader.

The next week, OSU turned in a tidy 21–6 win over Oregon despite six turnovers. The wheels were in motion. "We were in kind of a discovery mode," said Tatum. "We knew we were good, we just didn't know how good. Every week was a new experience."

It was time to grow up quickly however in week three, an October 12 date versus number one Purdue. The Buckeyes had been bombed by Mike Phipps, Leroy Keyes, and the rest of the Boilermakers the year before and loaded up with a defensive game plan devised by McCullough and first-year secondary coach Lou Holtz that included many defensive adjustments against the pass. The tone was set after a scoreless first half when Provost, flopping defensive positions with Tatum, stepped in front of an out pass by Phipps and ran untouched for a 35-yard TD that sent Ohio Stadium into a frenzy. Provost's spot was termed a "robber" in McCullough's system. That's exactly what he was.

With the defense frustrating Purdue and Otis leading the ground attack, all the Buckeyes needed was a knockout punch. They got it from an unlikely source. After Kern jammed his shoulder on a quarterback keeper, Hayes summoned reserve Bill Long, an all-but-forgotten senior who was often an outlet for criticism by OSU fans.

Not a great athlete, Long dropped back, didn't see anyone open, and took off on a 14-yard scoring run. The Buckeyes finished their masterpiece with more tight defense in the fourth quarter and held on for a 13–0 win.

Woody called the shutout, "The greatest defensive effort I've ever seen." No one disagreed.

After a 45–21 win over Northwestern, it finally was time to take the show on the road. OSU opened up a 24–0 lead in the third quarter at Illinois and then nearly frittered away an undefeated season.

"There were guys taking tape off and all that crap," Otis recalled.

But the game turned quickly as the 0–5 Illini scored three straight times and added three two-point conversions to tie the game and ignite the Homecoming crowd.

OSU fans didn't expect to miss Bill Long (24) behind center in 1968 but hailed him after he put away the upset of number one Purdue with an unlikely rushing touchdown. (courtesy The Ohio State University)

Then Kern got his bell rung. Hayes had called for Long and was about to shove him into the game when he changed his mind.

"No, goddammit, gimme Maciejowski," he said.

Maciejowski remembers his response: "Oh, sh __."

Luckily for the sophomore from Bedford, Ohio, he didn't have time to be nervous, not even when Foley greeted him in the huddle by saying, "Don't screw it up."

A fine athlete in his own right, Maciejowski didn't.

Faced with second and 17, he fired a 10-yard strike to Zelina, then picked up the first down with a nifty run to midfield. Now feeling his oats, "Mace" called a play in the huddle, a post to Zelina. He hit his classmate in stride for 44 yards and first and goal. The Buckeyes pounded it in from there and escaped with a 31–24 victory.

Kern continued to fight injuries and Maciejowski kept playing well in relief. He had a hand in a 25–20 squeaker over sixteenth-ranked Michigan State and a 43–8 blowout of Wisconsin in Madison.

In the eighth game of the season, Kern was back in full command and, for the most part, so was the Buckeye defense. Their assignment was to try to slow down Iowa tailback Ed Podolak, a former quarterback who had crushed the Big Ten single-game rushing record the previous week with 286 yards against Northwestern. Amazingly, he did it on only seventeen carries.

OSU ganged up on Podolak, opened up a 12–0 lead, got TDs from Kern and Brockington in the second half, and held off a furious rally to post a 33–27 win in Iowa City.

"Everything was hitting stride and we had Michigan left, which was a big game," Tatum said. "We knew we needed to make a statement."

Two Big Ones Left

Coaches always talk about peaking at the right time, and that's exactly what the Buckeyes did on November 23, 1968.

"We didn't need anyone ranting and raving and telling us 'This is what you play for.' We knew it," Zelina said. "We were able to turn off the outside distractions and had a very businesslike week of preparation."

The result was a monumental 50–14 win before a then-stadium record crowd of 85,371.

The score was actually tied at fourteen when OSU went on an 86-yard scoring march late in the first half. That came after Zelina's 59-yard kickoff return was called back because of a penalty. Otis capped the drive with a 2-yard TD.

The second half was pure heaven for Michigan haters as the Buckeyes scored twenty-nine unanswered points. OSU was able to dominate at the line of scrimmage as the result of a ploy to move the team's two All-American tackles, Foley and Mayes, to the right side of the formation. Assistant coaches Hugh Hindman and Earle Bruce sold the idea to Hayes.

"We started to run right over them," Kern said. "Then we ran the Counter 8 and the Counter 9 where we'd pull both guards and the corner wasn't ready for all that. That really threw them."

Hayes reinserted Otis for the final climactic touchdown to put OSU at the magic fifty-point mark. He then went for a two-point conversion, which failed. "I walked up to Woody and said, 'Coach, do you want that touchdown?,' and he said, 'Yeah, go in and get it,' " Otis said.

Otis was not only the toast of the town, in an odd way he had repeated history. In 1961 the Buckeyes also rolled up fifty points on Michigan and fullback Bob Ferguson, who would finish a close second to Syracuse's Ernie Davis in the Heisman balloting that year, scored four TDs in the rout. He gave his chinstrap to a Buckeye fan at Michigan Stadium after the game.

Seven years later, at the Friday night pep rally before "The Game," the same fan's son gave the chinstrap to Otis, who taped the good luck charm to his shoulder pad before also burning the Wolverines. His four TDs gave him sixteen on the year. That broke Howard "Hopalong" Cassady's team record of fifteen.

Rex Kern (10) hands off to fullback Jim Otis (35), a common sight in 1968. (Brockway Sports Photos)

The battering of number four Michigan in 1968 was so thorough, it even satisfied Hayes. He called it, "The best victory we ever had."

Fans tore down the goalposts and began an impromptu parade down High Street that reached the capitol building in the heart of downtown. There's no way to measure what the blowout did for the program considering the context of the season, town morale, and the impact on wide-eyed recruits.

John Hicks, who went on to become an All-American offensive lineman and Heisman Trophy runner-up in 1973, was in the stands that day as a recruit from Cleveland. "If you were from Ohio and didn't want to go there after that game, you weren't a Buckeye," he said.

Things weren't as rosy in Ann Arbor. Following the hard-to-swallow loss, Michigan moved longtime coach Bump Elliott up to an administrative position. Taking his place was Bo Schembechler, Woody's former player, assistant coach, and now a new rival.

While change was taking place up north in Michigan, the Buckeyes prepared for a trip to sunny California. To earn the third national championship of the Hayes era, the Buckeyes were going to have to win the Rose Bowl, which featured undefeated teams for the first time in the twenty-two-year history of the Big Ten–Pac 8 agreement. Meeting up with OSU in Pasadena was 9–0–1 Southern Cal and Heisman Trophy winner O. J. Simpson, a supremely gifted tailback who perfectly fit the USC running style.

Ironically, Ohio State, which was ranked number two for six straight weeks, moved up to the top spot with the convincing win over Michigan, jumping USC. But that was all a matter of opinion. The real issue was to be decided in possibly the greatest setting for a college football game.

OSU had played in four previous Rose Bowls against teams from the West Coast and won the last three: a 17–14 win over Cal that capped the 1949 season, a 20–7 win over USC that secured the 1954 national title, and a 10–7 triumph over Oregon in the 1958 Rose Bowl that returned OSU to the throne for the 1957 season. But eleven years later, the Buckeyes looked like tourists at the Disneyland information booth in the early going, falling into a 10–0 hole.

The Trojans opened the scoring with a chip-shot field goal in the second quarter and staggered OSU moments later when Simpson took a pitchout, reversed his field, and raced by everyone for an 80-yard touchdown.

It was time to get busy.

"Our offensive line was dominating SC's defensive line, but we weren't clicking on all cylinders yet," Kern said. "I went in the huddle and told the guys, 'OK, we've screwed around long enough. Let's start playing football.' "

What ensued was the same calm determination and domination that led OSU to its Big Ten title as the Buckeyes marched to their first touchdown, a drive capped by a 1-yard plunge by Otis. In fact, after OSU tied the score before halftime, took a 13–10 lead in the third quarter, and shocked USC with a pair of TD tosses by Kern, the Buckeyes had completed a 27–0 run that put them in total control.

On one key sequence Simpson was stymied inside the OSU 5.

"I still remember this vividly. I can see it in my mind," Tatum said. "They hit O. J. on a swing pass and I was able to catch him and knock him out on the 3. I took the tackle for a second because I thought he was the tight end, and then I saw where the play was going. We had to come up big there at the goal line, and we did. Mike Sensibaugh made three sensational tackles in a row."

Simpson finished with 171 yards rushing on twenty-eight carries. He also was USC's leading receiver with eight catches for 85 yards. Still, he was so impressed with the Buckeyes that he headed to their locker room after the game to tell them, "You're the best ballclub in the country and don't let anybody else tell you you aren't."

Many players on the team believe they found a second gear in the Rose Bowl because Hayes let them wear white mesh practice jerseys. The team warmed up in the California sun and knew they'd be overheated in their normal thick whites, which were made to endure freezing Midwest temperatures. The mesh jerseys would become a symbol of the team just like the buckeye leaves on the helmets, the black numerals on the sleeves of the home scarlet jerseys, and the diamond-shaped patterns in the Ohio Stadium end zones.

After the Rose Bowl, Hayes headed off to Vietnam to greet American troops, but not before he had a terse meeting with his coaching staff telling them none of them would be receiving a raise. The thirty-one-year-old Holtz, who was Woody's whipping boy for much of the season, decided to accept a position as the new head coach at William & Mary.

Holtz's move broke up what is still considered the greatest coaching staff in school history and one of the best of all time at the collegiate level. Four assistants went on to be successful head coaches: Holtz, who has led five different schools to bowl games and won the 1988 national championship at Notre Dame; Bruce, Hayes's successor at OSU and now in the College Football Hall of Fame; Bill Mallory, still considered by many the finest coach ever at Indiana; and George Chaump, a longtime mentor at Navy.

National Championships That Got Away

The following is a look at Ohio State football teams that just missed winning a national title:

1944: The Buckeyes go 9–0 under first-year coach Carroll Widdoes but finish second in the final Associated Press poll to Army.

1961: OSU (8–0–1) comes in second in the AP and United Press International polls when its administration declines a Rose Bowl invitation.

1969: Everything is in place for a repeat title but OSU (8–1), ranked number one all season long, is surprised by rival Michigan, 24–12.

1970: Another bitter pill for the Super Sophs as they lose to Stanford 27–17 in the Rose Bowl in their final game. The Buckeyes (9–1) settle for fifth and second, respectively, in the AP and UPI polls.

1973: Top-rated OSU ties Michigan 10–10 and finishes second in the AP poll despite blasting USC in the Rose Bowl. A 10–0–1 record is not good enough.

1975: The Buckeyes figure to close out the Archie Griffin era in style but lose hold of their number one ranking in a 23–10 upset by UCLA in the Rose Bowl.

1979: OSU (11–1) rips right through the Big Ten in Earle Bruce's first year at the helm, but the nation's top-ranked team is clipped in the final minutes by USC in the Rose Bowl, 17–16, settling for a number four ranking in both major polls.

1996: The number two Buckeyes blow a 9–0 halftime lead in a 13–9 home loss to Michigan. A thrilling defeat of Arizona State in the Rose Bowl still leaves OSU (11–1) second in the polls.

1998: Ohio State is threatening to go wire to wire as number one until a fateful November visit from Michigan State and a stunning 28–24 loss. OSU finishes 11–1 and second in the polls again.

The 1968 Buckeyes lived on in OSU lore, especially after the same core group neared but failed to grab another title in 1969 and 1970. "The irony of all the talk over the years about 1968 is we always felt as players the best team we had was 1969," Otis said. "But when you lose to Michigan, that gets forgotten in a hurry."

Added Zelina: "We still talk about what could have been whenever we get together. We should have won three consecutive national championships."

Kern agreed with that regret but added: "When you look back on it and see what's happened since, and how hard it is to win it, I think we have to feel fortunate to win the one we did. That outweighs any disappointment for me."

Time proved that the 1968 team was indeed special. With the Big Ten developing into a more balanced conference in the 1980s and then adding traditional Eastern power Penn State in the 1990s, running the table has become nearly impossible. The only Big Ten teams to post undefeated, untied seasons after 1968 were Penn State in 1994 (which finished second in the major polls) and Michigan in 1997 (which topped the Associated Press poll).

For thirty-four years no Big Ten team could win an undisputed national crown. Then came 2002 and a new band of Buckeye champions.

Jim Tressel: "A Real Cool Cat"

There are dozens of those snake-oil salesman types who inundate sports bettors with their "guaranteed winners" for the big game, and then there's Mark Summers, who *knew* Jim Tressel was going to be standing on the makeshift winner's platform after the 2003 Fiesta Bowl.

Oh sure, the 50,000-plus Ohio State fans in the stands of Sun Devil Stadium and the entirety of central Ohio will tell you now that they were "feeling good" about the chances of the Buckeyes, who were as much as thirteen-point underdogs against mighty Miami (Florida).

And Summers?

"I had no doubt," said the Cleveland money manager, who happens to be Tressel's best friend.

Summers had more reason than most to be confident. He has seen Tressel in just about every pressure-cooker situation of his adult life—including Tressel's days as the field general at Baldwin-Wallace—and more often than not his cool and calm paid off big-time.

In his previous head coaching gig at Youngstown State, Tressel won four Division 1-AA national championships in fifteen years.

"It was the same thing there," Summers said. "He was the same guy; he built things up the same way with the same brand of football. They would play teams like Marshall and

A former quarterback, Tressel assesses every last detail on game day.
(Jeff Brehm)

The Citadel and Eastern Washington in big games and people would say 'That power I is not going to work this time' and 'they have way too much speed,' and I'd watch [YSU] just go out and whack these teams because they were so fine-tuned at the end of the season.

"When he was getting ready to play Miami and all you heard about was the thirty-four-game winning streak and the team speed and how overmatched Ohio State was, all I could think was, 'This is going to be déjà vu.' "

It may have seemed that way to Summers, but the majority of the country was skeptical, partly because Tressel supposedly was in over his head. But after the Buckeyes pulled off a shocker and grabbed the program's first national championship since 1968, about the only thing over Tressel's head was a halolike glow. He joined Paul Brown and Woody Hayes as the only coaches to lead OSU all the way to the promised land. Not bad company.

After leading OSU to an unprecedented 14–0 season, Tressel ended up sweeping all the major coach of the year awards, including the one presented by the Football Writers Association of America, which dates back to 1957, when Hayes claimed the honor after leading the Buckeyes to a national title.

Tressel also was recognized by the American Football Coaches Association, making him the first coach to win the AFCA award at two different schools (he was twice honored at Youngstown State) and joining him with his late father, Lee, as the first father-son tandem to be named coach of the year.

Chip Off the Old Block

Being the son of Lee and Eloise, high school sweethearts in Ada, Ohio, gave James Patrick Tressel the ideal smarts, experience, and temperament he needed to succeed as a coach. An Ohio boy born in Mentor, Jim grew up in Massillon and later Berea, where his father was the well-regarded head coach at Baldwin-Wallace. The practice field was within view of the Tressels' backyard. Eloise would ring a bell for dinner in the off-season because Jim and his older brothers, Dick and Dave, often hung out there.

Jim also used to frequent the Cleveland Browns' training site. Lee would pop by to see his good friend, Lou "The Toe" Groza.

"His dad used to stop by our practices and little Jimmy used to shag balls, help out however he could," said lineman Jim Houston, who starred at both Ohio State and Cleveland. "He was a very pleasant young kid."

It was an idyllic life, but one based on poise and hard work. Jim's grandfather worked in the fields of his farm in his eighties. Lee, who often wore a bow tie and a brush cut, was the consummate worker as a coach. Jim learned from their constant example.

A handsome honor student, Jim also became the top athlete at Berea High School. The decision about which college to attend was simple. He played for his father and became an all-conference quarterback.

It was at Baldwin-Wallace where Tressel, the straight-laced quarterback, befriended Summers, a linebacker who liked to live life a little bit more on the edge. Despite their differences number 7 and number 42 were inseparable. They roomed together on the road, were fraternity brothers at Alpha Tau Omega, and were named senior cocaptains in 1974.

"Jim was a very, very bright guy, a great student," Summers said. "And he was always for the team. Being a captain with him and playing for his dad [are among] the most honorable things I've done in my life. You know why? Because they're great people. His mom was an awesome lady, too. Just

The Tressels had the look of a classic 1950s family when Jim (seated top left) was a six-year-old lad. (courtesy Dick Tressel)

extremely consistent people who never got too upset about anything.

"Jim is just like everyone else in his family. What you see is what you get. There's no phoniness and never any panic. He's a quality Christian man, but a competitor, too. Don't mix that up."

Jim also inherited a love of Ohio State from his parents, who both attended school there. Lee was a promising back in the 1940s, even starring in the spring scrimmage. But his career in scarlet and gray was cut short when he left school to serve in World War II.

Once a year, Jim would watch the Buckeyes on television with his father and root for his dad's alma mater. "Typically my dad's season was over and the Ohio State–Michigan game was the first time we had a chance to sit down and do anything with him," he said.

Jim eventually made it to his dad's old haunts, earning a job as an assistant coach under Earle Bruce at OSU in 1983. He was put in charge of the quarterbacks and wide receivers, and the following year he also gained responsibility for the running backs. That paid immediate dividends—Keith Byars was named MVP of the Big Ten and runner-up for the Heisman Trophy and OSU advanced to the Rose Bowl. In his three years under Bruce, Tressel also developed talents Cris Carter and Mike Tomczak.

"He had great attention to detail and that's what was motivating," Byars said. "He'd see the little things you could have done better, whether it was how your foot was turned, how you blocked, or whatever, and that made you want to be a better player."

Now entrenched as the head coach, Tressel has shown he is hands-on with all his players. Despite being meticulous and on an even keel, he often is compared with Hayes by idealistic fans who believe the head coach should win every game and make an admirable man out of every player.

"I see some similarities," said Archie Griffin, who was a standout under Hayes and had a hand in the hiring of Tressel. "Jim has got a plan, and his plan has worked—probably ahead of time. Jim is involved in every facet of game preparation and so was Woody, especially in the offense. You'd see him in the huddle calling the plays.

"But the thing that sticks out is the caring. Jim cares about the kids, he wants them to be successful. He cares about their

Ohio State's Head Coaches

Jim Tressel became Ohio State's twenty-second head football coach when he was hired in 2001. The school began to play recorded intercollegiate football in 1890, with Alexander S. Lilley serving as the program's original coach. Including Lilley and spanning to John Richards in 1912, OSU had 11 different head coaches. Here's a list of the next 11 coaches who have directed OSU since it joined what is now the Big Ten Conference, and their all-time records at the school:

John Wilce (1913–28): 78-33-9 (.688)
Sam Willaman (1929–33): 26-10-5 (.695)
Francis Schmidt (1934–40): 39-16-1 (.705)
Paul Brown (1941–43): 18-8-1 (.685)
Carroll Widdoes (1944–45): 16-2 (.889)
Paul Bixler (1946): 4-3-2 (.556)
Wes Fesler (1947–50): 21-13-3 (.608)
Woody Hayes (1951–78): 205-61-10 (.761)
Earle Bruce (1979–87): 81-26-1 (.755)
John Cooper (1988–2000): 111-43-4 (.715)
Jim Tressel (2001–02): 21-5 (.808)

families; he cares about them getting out in the communities and being involved.

"A lot of that had to do with his own father. They may call him Little Woody but his father had those attributes, too."

Indeed, the day Tressel first spoke to the media as OSU head coach, he talked mostly about his concerns and hopes for the student-athletes, a trait handed down from Lee. "The thing that he taught me most was that he cared about every person," Tressel said.

"It's his old man," said former OSU star lineman John Hicks, who was recruited by Tressel's father. "It's the same thing. You can see the importance he puts on how he treats people and the community. He's an old-fashioned football coach. His dad didn't jump from job to job. He built the thing up. Jim wants to be the same way. That's all he wants to do."

Sometimes Tressel feels like he is still trying to live up to the legacy of his dad, who won a national title at B-W in 1978 (he died from lung cancer in his mid-fifties just three years later) and was inducted into the College Football Hall of Fame in 1996.

Jim spent his fiftieth birthday at a dinner honoring Bruce for also making the College Football Hall of Fame. While at the dais, Michigan's former coach Bo Schembechler looked at the man who had just beaten UM for the second straight year and said, "Jim Tressel has done a marvelous job. He's still not the coach his daddy was. He's got to do a little work there."

Ironically, after the 2002 win over Michigan, Tressel's career record at YSU and OSU combined was 155–62–2. Lee's mark in twenty-three years at B-W was 155–52–6. Jim passed his pop with Ohio State's epic victory in the Fiesta Bowl by sticking to some tried-and-true football maxims—attack on defense, play smart on offense, and win the turnover margin.

Lee's teams actually were way more wide open, with multiple formations and misdirection plays. He employed two wingbacks, put receivers in motion, and ordered his QB to spread the wealth and keep defenses honest. In fact Lee was a confidant of run-and-shoot guru Mouse Davis.

But the rest of Lee was Ward Cleaver all the way, and it rubbed off on Jim, who issues pop quizzes to players, asking them the hometowns and high schools of their teammates; carries around a notebook with inspirational messages; and can calculate at any moment how many days until the Buckeyes play Michigan.

How 1950s is Tressel? On Saturday he wears a cotton sweater vest and a tie, even when he has short sleeves underneath. It's as if he has to sweep up at Johnny Rockets after the game.

He looks to put his players on the spot by shifting questions directed at him to them. If they don't stop to sign autographs or if they do anything untoward in public, he lets them know about it. If they don't look clean cut, he needles them. At the media luncheon he once jabbed punter Andy Groom for once again wearing his "Don Johnson outfit."

Of course, Athletic Director Andy Geiger is just as thrilled with the squeaky clean image as he is with the winning, especially after citing a "deteriorating climate" when he fired John Cooper in January of 2001. "To my way of thinking, Jim Tressel represents the very best there is, both as a coach and as a person," Geiger said. "We are fortunate to have him as our head coach."

Rock Steady

A "trestle" is described by Noah Webster, more or less, as a beam used as a support.

That also would be an appropriate way to describe Jim Tressel, who arrived on the head-coaching scene with a very strong base. He graduated cum laude from Baldwin-Wallace in 1975 with a degree in education and had his sights set on joining Joe Paterno's staff at Penn State. Lee, however, thought his son was getting too starry-eyed and set it up for him to go to Akron instead.

As a twenty-two-year-old grad student at Akron, Jim's duties included teaching six classes on campus, handling game film, running the weight room, and serving as a resident assistant. He also had the role of quarterbacks coach, unheard of for a grad assistant.

Tressel became a full-fledged assistant for the Zips, serving in Akron until 1978. He spent the next two years at Miami (Ohio), the "Cradle of Coaches," as a QB/receivers coach. That led to a two-year stint as QB coach at Syracuse and the three-year gig at Ohio State.

At OSU, Tressel had the same fire as assistants Glen Mason, Gary Blackney, and Dom Capers, who all went on to be head coaches. He also learned under the tutelage of Earle Bruce, which he labeled, "One of my greatest blessings."

Tressel marveled at the honesty and determination of Bruce. "The thing that I learned so much from him is you can't be a great coach unless you're tough. Earle Bruce was tough," he said.

No one was surprised when Tressel's name began to surface as a head-coaching candidate. He grabbed at the chance to rebuild Youngstown State. Tressel was just 2–9 in his first year in Youngstown (1986) but eventually pulled the Penguins out of their slide.

Summers recalls what he terms "the turning point in Jim's coaching career." It came in 1991. Youngstown State was just

Skepticism Comes with the Whistle

When Andy Geiger set out to find a replacement for John Cooper, whom he fired as Ohio State head football coach on January 2, 2001, he looked into bringing in some high-priced talent. Eventually, he settled on Jim Tressel, a former OSU assistant who was running a nice little program up at Youngstown State. This was not met with great praise at first, but these things rarely are.

After the hiring, typifying the reaction, Tim Sullivan, a columnist for the *Cincinnati Enquirer* wrote, "Jim Tressel must feel like a provisional prom date. He's the guy who gets the girl if the girl can't find anybody better. He's a fallback position, an insurance policy, a stooge. . . . Shouldn't Ohio State's search committee, scouring the country for an ideal candidate, be able to attract someone with a higher profile than Division 1-AA Youngstown State?"

Having to answer harsh criticism even before you've coached your first game in Columbus comes with the territory. Once referred to as "The Graveyard of Coaches," Ohio State is not exactly for the meek anyway. Alumni and the media often sour on the OSU coach after a while, making them leery of the next hire.

When Earle Bruce was brought on in 1979, many OSU fans already had fantasies of getting another former OSU assistant, Lou Holtz. Bruce found a way to win them over, though. His first team went 11–0 in the regular season and played for the national championship. Still, "Old 9–3 Earle" often left followers thirsting for more wins.

In 1951, despite the public's interest in getting an Ohio man and a spirited campaign to "Bring Back Brown"—referring to Paul Brown, briefly an OSU coach and an Ohio coaching legend—the Ohio State brass decided on a well-regarded outsider in Don Faurot. But on returning to Missouri and imagining the pressure cooker he was about to enter, Faurot reconsidered. As a result Ohio State hired Woody Hayes, the head coach at Miami (Ohio) and a former ship commander in the Navy.

When Hayes's T-formation offense sputtered in the 1951 opener, a record Ohio Stadium crowd made Hayes feel welcome—with a chorus of boos.

4–3 and faced with playing at powerful Georgia Southern, one of the most intimidating places to play in Division 1-AA. The game had a must-win feel.

"Four losses and you don't go to the playoffs," Summers said.

He stood on the sideline and watched the Penguins chew up the last five minutes of the game with a ball-control drive that included Tressel going for a pair of fourth and 1s inside his own 40.

"If he punts, he loses, and he knows it," Summers said. "They win to go 5–3 and they run the table."

The Penguins claimed a national title with a win over Marshall, and Tressel received state and national awards as coach of the year. Titles followed in 1993, 1994, and 1997. By 1999 Tressel had pocketed four rings in six appearances in the national title game.

Tressel also became athletic director at YSU and used his power to improve facilities, encourage students to get involved in the community, and aid charitable causes. Over time he became one of the most revered figures in the Mahoning Valley.

But when he became a candidate for the job at OSU along with coaches such as Walt Harris and his old buddy Glen Mason, he admitted being interested. "Anyone from Ohio would be lying if they said they weren't," he said.

Tressel then knocked Geiger's socks off in his interview, demonstrating a plan for every facet of the program. He was hired after OSU tinkered with the idea of wooing Oklahoma's Bob Stoops, Oregon's Mike Bellotti, and NFL hot property Jon Gruden. Tressel's base salary jumped from $85,000 to $700,000.

Although the people in Youngstown understood, the town basically went into a state of mourning.

"You do all these checks. Everybody spoke so highly of him," said Griffin, who as associate athletic director served on the search committee. "We all liked his record, which was just fantastic, and certainly the four national championships get your attention.

"But the fact that he talked about the players and things that he wanted them to be involved with—he talked not only about the football part of it but the community involvement—I think that had a lot to do with him being selected.

"You couldn't find anybody who had a bad thing to say about Jim Tressel."

Leader of the Family

The day that Tressel was introduced as Ohio State's new head coach in January 2001 he dazzled the media and public with an immaculate and thorough address that touched on everything from his theories on coaching to his deep-rooted beliefs in community involvement.

Later that night, he spoke one of the most well-received sentences ever uttered by any OSU coach. He told a packed Schottenstein Center on hand to see the OSU–Michigan basketball game, "I can assure you, you will be proud of our young people in the classroom, in the community, and, most especially, in 310 days in Ann Arbor, Michigan, on the football field."

OSU fans liked the fact that Tressel was Ohio born and bred and that he understood the importance of beating Michigan instead of playing down the rivalry, which Cooper often did. Still, there was much reservation about bringing in a small-college guy—but not from those who knew him well.

"I think they got a great coach. I knew that right away,"

Tressel acknowledges the crowd at the Schottenstein Center during his now-famous "310 days" speech. (Steve Helwagen/Buckeye Sports Bulletin)

Bruce said. "I visited him at the 1-AA program and that program was run like any big-time program you've ever seen. And they were a little ahead of some of the big-time programs with what they were doing with academics up there, for sure."

Tressel's coaching debut came on September 8, 2001, against Akron, the very school at which he'd started out as a coach. His mother died just before the start of fall camp. But even with all the hoopla and emotions burning inside of him, he made sure to follow his father's lead around his players: Show them you care; stay consistent.

Tressel's demeanor is so controlled that it's news when he

The caring approach learned from his father resonates with Tressel's players, even the brash Maurice Clarett. *(Jeff Brehm)*

pumps his fist or raises his voice on game day. When OSU was in position to claim the national championship in Arizona, longtime OSU beat writer Rusty Miller of the Associated Press chuckled and said, "Pouring a bucket of ice water on this guy brings his temperature *up*."

But it's no coincidence that the Buckeyes were able to overcome high-pressure situations in that 2002 season with Tressel staying composed on the sideline. Cooper, whose teams sometimes faltered in such situations, often was a ball of nerves who would chomp on his fingernails and gripe at the side judge when matters were tense and stakes were high.

"I've always believed in football your team gets its personality from the head coach," said Byars, who had a lengthy career in the NFL. "Jim Tressel is such a cool customer that he doesn't panic and you see that with his teams.

"I think that fiery coach stuff is overrated. I mean, Bill Parcells was one of the best motivational coaches I had and he never gave us a rah-rah speech."

Added running back Maurice Hall, one of Tressel's first recruits at OSU: "It definitely helps you out because if you're nervous, you don't want your coach walking around like he's nervous. It definitely helps us to stay calm and comfortable and just focus."

One of many Buckeyes recruited to OSU by Cooper, wide receiver Michael Jenkins said it didn't take long for Tressel to ingratiate himself with just about everyone. "Coach Tressel is a special guy," he said. "Everybody loves him in Youngstown and everybody loves him here now. To gain that already is just remarkable. He's a real cool cat."

Even before OSU closed the 2002 season with historic wins over Michigan and Miami, offensive lineman Alex Stepanovich said Tressel had improved the outlook and mission of the program.

"When you have a leader like Coach Tress . . . the way he carries himself, you do take on that personality. He's the quintessential great guy. He focuses on everything he has to focus on. I mean, he stresses family, he stresses school, and that's the way our team has approached it. We realize it's a privilege to play here and respecting that privilege that he's told us about and shown us has kind of made us take a part of what he is.

"He always fights, and when you respect a guy like him you want to fight for a guy like him."

And when a coach gets that kind of group result at a place like Ohio State, special things follow.

"We had our forty-fifth reunion [during the 2002 season]," Houston said, "and a lot of us started talking about how much we like Coach Tressel and the positive spin he has put on things here. He makes no bones about it: You're here to get an education, you're here to play football, and you have to carry yourself the right way in both endeavors.

"What I like the most when I watch games is I see his kids play with class and they play hard. If you get whipped, you get whipped, and you don't make excuses.

"I think there's an aura around the program again."

Still the Grandest of Them All

About an hour and a half after Ohio State had defeated Michigan on November 23, 2002, a game some labeled the program's biggest home game ever, I made sure to stop and look around the confines of Ohio Stadium. This is something I've done many times, always with wonderment. It's something just about every OSU fan has done, too.

The Horseshoe. Being in it is like visiting an old friend. I've seen it empty and staid. I've also seen it as a powder keg of emotion for an entire community. I've howled in it, frozen in it, let loose all feelings of joy in the stands, and pumped my fist once or twice under the table in the press box. I've also felt sick to my stomach in it, seen seasons of greatness sour in one blink of the eye.

I still marvel at the majesty of the stadium and how it pulls me into focus whether as a frenetic, jam-packed setting on game day or as an awe-inspiring, world-class edifice. I'm not ashamed to say I've walked into the stadium and had my eyes mist up. I'm not ashamed to say it because I know many others have experienced the same thing.

Sometimes it's almost eerie to trek through the south end zone after participating in postgame interviews in the southeast tower. The walk back to the press box usually is in darkness, through debris, and in the eerie quiet of an almost empty stadium, a whole world away from the Roman-like feel of the place during games.

I guess I've used the 'Shoe to fit and shape my mood. I make a point of going down on the field before every game I cover. One of my favorite moments is watching the eyes of young recruits turn into saucers as the Ohio State Marching Band enters the field level. No seventeen-year-old is emotionally prepared for that. I usually take in the band, listen to them play "Carmen Ohio," and watch the team run onto the field before I head up to my lofty little perch in the press box. If my life has become too mundane or my job has become too exhausting that week, the pregame festivities almost always manage to put some fire back in my belly.

The postgame effect is more serene but sometimes just as powerful. After OSU took care of Michigan and wrapped up a BCS title game berth, fans within a mile radius were celebrating, delirious with victory and thoughts of the Fiesta Bowl. But I stood and looked around at the battle-worn field that had been home to eight games that season, all wins. I noticed a chunk of sod was missing right about where Maurice Hall scored the game-winning touchdown. Some people had dug up turf at the painted numbers, too, probably because it corresponded to their seats in the stands. The goalposts were still intact but wobbly after attempts by students to rock them to the ground.

History, yet again, had been written in the 'Shoe, and I got to breathe it in. But I am not alone. Summed up Ohio State poet laureate David Citino, a longtime season ticket holder who once read a poem he wrote in the stadium in tribute to the late Woody Hayes, "Walking through the darkness out a tunnel and looking out on a field, it hits you how many great and terrible things have happened in that place. So many incredible contests."

Ohio Stadium Quick Facts

- First game: versus Ohio Wesleyan on October 7, 1922
- Dedication: versus Michigan on October 21, 1922
- Original cost: $1,341,017
- Renovation cost (1999–2001): approximately $210 million
- Original capacity: 66,210
- Current capacity: 101,568
- Largest crowd: 105,539 (versus Michigan on November 23, 2002)
- All-time attendance: more than thirty-five million
- All-time OSU record in the stadium: 346–103–20 (through 2002)
- Original surface: grass
- Prescription athletic turf installed: 1990
- Stadium length: 919 feet
- Stadium width: 679 feet
- Height of press box roof: 183 feet, 4 inches (from field level)
- Suites: 81

To Citino the stadium is a personal time capsule as he has vivid memories of being there with his children. "My memories of the stadium often involve sitting there with my kids at various stages of their lives," he said. "There was incredible elation and heartbreak when we lost. There's just something about the sights and even the smells when you're sitting in those stands."

Raymont Harris was a prized recruit out of Lorain, Ohio, when he made his first trek to Columbus to see a game in 1988. Not ready for such a massive structure, Harris went to the wrong gate and was not allowed in by ushers, despite an invitation from the coaching staff. Meanwhile inside, the Buckeyes forged a sensational comeback and defeated LSU. "I was pissed," he recalled. "I remember saying, 'I'm never going to Ohio State.'"

Ohio Field circa 1909 (courtesy The Ohio State University)

But Harris did return for a visit and once he saw the Horseshoe from the inside, his feelings changed fast. He, of course, committed to the Buckeyes and won the Silver Football Award as MVP of the Big Ten in 1993.

Longtime recruiting coordinator Bill Conley believes the stadium is the program's best recruiting tool. "We always feel that if we can get a young man on campus and show him around, we've got an excellent chance to land him," Conley said. "The stadium plays a major role in that. We'll bring kids out to midfield and have them look around at the stands during their visit. Then we'll announce their name over the loudspeaker and put it up on the scoreboard. That's a powerful moment for a young kid. We've gotten a lot of players that way."

One of them was Keith Byars.

"I remember the first time I walked inside the stadium," said Byars, a Dayton native who became a record-setting tailback for OSU in 1984. "I looked at the hallowed ground and thought of all the great players that were there before me who built up the great tradition. It just made me appreciate the opportunity and want to make every experience as special as it could be inside that place."

And twenty years after running out of the south tunnel for the first time, Byars felt chills again as he lined up on the middle of the field along with many other former players to greet the Buckeyes as they raced onto the sod for the 2002 game with Michigan. The formation is called the Tunnel of Pride.

"To go out on the field like that, a piece of me still wants to run out there," he said. "I was ready to hit somebody."

The home field is special to just about any football player, but at Ohio State the tradition behind the program and the aura around the stadium itself go way beyond the norm.

Ohio State recognizes the birth of its program as 1890, although students played games as far back as 1881 near the old North Dorm, an area that now serves as a courtyard near the University Hospitals. A fence and bleachers to hold 200 were built in 1892. Play shifted to University Field, just west of High Street and south of Woodruff Avenue, in 1898. It was renamed Ohio Field in 1908 and could seat around 14,000.

Interest grew when OSU joined the Western Conference in 1913, but Ohio State football didn't really take flight until the arrival of Charles "Chic" Harley, who had packed in standing room only crowds at Columbus East High School. A superstar with pure all-around ability, Harley led the Buckeyes to conference championships in 1916 and 1917. He took the following year off from school because of military service but returned in 1919, when he led the Buckeyes to their first-ever win over Michigan. Ohio Field simply couldn't host the demand for seats anymore and the university began plans for Ohio Stadium, which some dubbed, "The House That Harley Built."

Harley Was First Buckeye Icon

Way before there was Archie Griffin and Woody Hayes and even Les Horvath and Paul Brown at Ohio State, there was Charles W. "Chic" Harley, a man who single-handedly infused the OSU football craze with his dazzling skill, charming looks, and cool demeanor.

Harley was a modest 5'9" and 150 pounds but he was a true phenom. In fact there wasn't a sport he couldn't master. In football Harley was the quintessential punt, pass, and kick champion. He also was one of the best open-field runners the young game had seen.

Harley grew into stardom at Columbus East High School. After word of Harley's all-around brilliance on the gridiron spread, East repeatedly drew more fans to home games in 1914 than Ohio State did for its games at Ohio Field.

The Harley family with seven children did not have money to send Chic through college. But he was coaxed to OSU by head coach John Wilce, and as the story goes, he was provided free room and board by the Phi Gamma Delta fraternity.

By 1916 Harley was a twenty-year-old freshman sporting the leather helmet, high socks, belted pants, and striped sweatshirt of Ohio State. That year he led the Buckeyes to a 7–0 mark and its first conference title with several memorable performances, including a 7–6 win over mighty Illinois in which he scrambled for a touchdown and drop-kicked the game-winning conversion.

After the undefeated 1917, Harley joined the war effort and served in the Army Air Corps in 1918. He came back to OSU in 1919 and picked up where he left off with another outstanding season, which included a 13–3 win over rival Michigan in Ann Arbor, icing the victory with a breathtaking 42-yard touchdown, four interceptions, and eleven punts for a 42-yard average. (Prior to Harley's arrival OSU had lost all fifteen meetings with UM by a combined score of 369–21.)

The great Chic Harley.
(courtesy The Ohio State University)

Harley, in fact, won every game in his OSU career except his last, a heartbreaking 9–7 loss to Illinois. More than 20,000 people jammed into Ohio Field for the send-off. Illinois won on a late 25-yard field goal. Legend has it that Harley stayed up all night on the eve of the game walking the campus and stayed in the dressing room for hours after the loss.

Harley not only became OSU's first All-American, he soon was recognized as college football's greatest player. He led OSU to a 21–1–1 mark and two titles in three seasons and was named All-American after each campaign.

But Harley's most lasting accomplishment was his intense popularity, which led to plans for the construction of Ohio Stadium just months after his departure. Harley, a charter member of the College Football Hall of Fame, attended OSU's game with Michigan in 1922, when the new 70,000-seat structure was dedicated.

Some people still call it "The House That Harley Built."

The new stadium was designed in the summer of 1918 by university architect Howard Dwight Smith, who came up with a unique horseshoe-shaped double-decker look, the first of its kind in the world. Smith, who studied the Colosseum in Rome and the Parthenon in Athens during his training, wanted a classic house of competition. His work won a gold medal from the American Institute of Architects in 1921. (In 1974 Ohio Stadium was added to the National Registry of Historic Buildings.)

Building Ohio Stadium was no easy task, although the project was more-or-less completed thirteen months after the August 3, 1921, groundbreaking. Locomotive cranes with long booms lifted 4,500 tons of steel to erect the frame. About 85,000 tons of concrete made up the exterior and base for the stands. Almost two million feet of lumber was used as well. When complete, Ohio Stadium stood 98 feet high and was 725 feet long and 596 feet wide.

No one can deny its originality, beauty, or charm. Those close to the program also view it as a powerful, idyllic symbol of the football program, university, and state.

Longtime Ohio State coach John W. Wilce wrote an editorial about the stadium in 1919, three years before it was completed. Dr. Wilce's words proved prophetic when he wrote, "Students, alumni, faculty, and friends of our great Ohio State University have grown as they have made possible its practical construction. The stadium is not a monument, however, in its largest interpretation; it is a living stimulation toward the maintenance of strong, virile, clean, active elements in the broad field of education."

Ohio State had a recognizable and sturdy home for its beloved football team, but little was done in the way of preserving the stadium in the following decades. Even when the concrete began to show wear, renovation plans were scrapped

"The House That Harley Built" still needed some finishing touches in 1922.
(courtesy The Ohio State University)

in the 1970s and 1980s as the school tried to maintain its athletic budget. But when Andy Geiger attended his first home game as athletic director in 1994, he was stunned at some of the problems he saw.

For one, the stadium was not up to code. Also, it didn't have the modern amenities of many rival schools.

Geiger went to work on a massive three-year renovation plan that began in 1999 and included the following: lowering the playing field 14.6 feet to provide better sight lines and add seating, taking out the track that Jesse Owens once ran upon (the university has since built a track stadium in Owens's name), constructing permanent south stands, installing new concrete facades all the way around the outer structure, adding

The renovated and permanent South Stands make an even more intimidating backdrop for visitors. (Jeff Brehm)

luxury suites, designating seating and other accommodations for the handicapped, building a new team locker room, and adding a recruiting room and interview room in the southeast tower. Also, stained glass depictions of OSU football, one of them looking very much like Eddie George scoring a touchdown, were added to the north rotunda.

When the project was complete in 2001, the stadium grew in height by 38 feet, length by 215 feet, and width by 83 feet. With all those changes some, unfortunately, did take away from the structure's original charm. Nonetheless, the reviews were raves once Ohio Stadium was successfully modernized without the necessity of a complete facelift.

"What we always intended was to make necessary improvements to the structure but maintain the integrity of the stadium," Geiger said. "I feel that we did that."

The stadium—in its various configurations—has served many purposes over the years. It has hosted NFL preseason games; Ohio Glory World Football League games; Columbus Crew Major League Soccer matches; OSU track and field meets, including the Jesse Owens Classic; state high school football and track championships; Special Olympics; school commencements; and several concerts, including ones featuring the Rolling Stones, U2, Genesis, Billy Joel, Elton John, and Pink Floyd.

Today, the stadium features a scoreboard that is more than 25,000 square feet in area with newly enhanced acoustics.

But with its simple name, ideal on-campus setting on the banks of the Olentangy River, and historical appearance, it remains a beautiful, noncommercialized arena for athletics.

A Rivalry Like No Other

Anyone who is a fan or follower of Ohio State football has instant memories of OSU–Michigan games over the years. Many ardent fans can recall where a particular game was played, who won, and what the key plays were. The moments that led to defeat or victory are indelible.

Over the years I've interviewed countless players and coaches, even some Wolverines, on the subject of the OSU–Michigan game. The Game has so much meaning to them they sometimes struggle to put its meaning into words. Before the 1994 game former OSU tailback and broadcaster Jeff Logan addressed the team. While describing The Game's significance and pleading with the Buckeyes to stop a six-year winless streak, Logan's voice began to crack and tears rolled down his cheeks.

Recruits from out of state know about the rivalry and that both schools are traditional powers, but they don't grasp what's going on until they see a scene like that. "When you see a grown man crying talking about Michigan, it gets your attention," said former quarterback Stanley Jackson, a native of Paterson, New Jersey.

All-American safety Mike Doss was part of the 2001 and 2002 teams that were the first to win back-to-back games versus UM in twenty years. "It's a season within a season," he said. "This is totally different from any game you'll ever play. It means a lot for the community, for the youth out there who might . . . play for Ohio State and represent this side of the rivalry."

But why is it so important?

Trying to explain the phenomenon to an outsider is about like sending a Martian snapshots of life on Earth. You've got to be near it, be in it, or have a vested interest in it to get the full picture.

The theories on how to win this game vary widely: Keep it simple. Change things up. Don't get too engrossed in it. Treat it as the most important thing you've ever done in your life. Give the opponent your ultimate respect. Hate them. But all associated with The Game agree on one thing: It's the greatest rivalry in sports.

OSU–UM: Tighter Than You Think

You ask the average fan on the street outside Big Ten country who has had the better of the OSU–UM rivalry, and that fan likely will tell you Michigan, based on John Cooper's highly publicized failures in the series as OSU coach from 1988–2000. But the truth is Michigan's edge has more to do with the embryonic stage of the rivalry when the Wolverines went 13-0-2 in the first fifteen games in the series, posting, get this, eleven shutouts. The Buckeyes finally got a "W" In 1919 behind star halfback Chic Harley.

From the time spanning Woody Hayes's arrival in Columbus in 1951 until 2002, when Jim Tressel improved to 2-0 against "the school up north," the series was deadlocked at 25-25-2.

On November 22, 2003, Tressel's Buckeyes will look for a rare hat trick in what will be the one hundredth installment of the series.

May they play a hundred more.

It's also one of the great defining moments for an Ohio State football player, the coaching staff, the season, and, in all reality, the program itself—for lots of reasons.

For starters Ohio State and Michigan easily boast two of the most tradition-rich programs in college football. Through 2002, Michigan had won at least a share of forty Big Ten titles, easily the most in the conference. Ohio State was second with twenty-nine. Next was Minnesota with eighteen, although the last of those titles came in 1967. It's no wonder that the Big Ten used to be known as "The Big Two and The Little Eight." Each school has one of the top-ten winningest programs of all time. More often than not, Big Ten titles, national rankings, and even major awards such as the Heisman Trophy are hanging in the balance when the two teams meet. Sometimes a coach's job can be added to the list.

Plus, it's possible that no rivalry in the sport is more watched than Ohio State–Michigan, traditionally an ABC noon telecast in late November. As far as actual total attendance in the stands, OSU–UM has drawn more fans than any other rivalry since 1922, the year the Buckeyes moved into Ohio Stadium. The Wolverines play in Michigan Stadium, which has a capacity of 107,501, tops in the country. Ohio Stadium seats 101,568, fourth-largest of any college venue. It seems every year a new attendance record is set when the Buckeyes take on the Wolverines.

Also, the two schools, marquee universities in bordering states, seem to be intertwined. A lot of businesses or industries in one state have offices or subsidiaries in the other. My dad, for example, worked for Rockwell International in Columbus for two decades but was transferred to Detroit at the end of his career with the company.

Woody and Bo

They called it the Ten Year War. How else could you describe the best rivalry in sports at its fiercest—the ten times Woody Hayes–led Ohio State took on rival Michigan and the coach who learned his craft from Woody, Glenn "Bo" Schembechler?

In those classic matchups from 1969–78, the Big Ten Conference title was on the line every time. And that ten-year block of time started off with a bang.

Schembechler played under Hayes at Miami (Ohio) and was a graduate assistant and assistant coach of the junior varsity at Ohio State in 1951, not coincidentally Woody's first year in Columbus. Bo also was a full-fledged assistant at OSU from 1958–62.

But he will be known forever as a Michigan man. His long tenure in Ann Arbor began in 1969. Ohio State just so happened to enter Michigan Stadium that year undefeated and number one in the country. Because of the "no-repeat rule," OSU was not allowed to represent the conference in the Rose Bowl, meaning a repeat national title was at stake for the Buckeyes.

Schembechler was a rookie UM head coach, but he knew how to fuel the rivalry. He had the number 50 taped to the jersey of all his scout players in preparation for the game, a reminder of OSU's 50–14 shellacking in Ohio Stadium the year before.

"I made sure that those guys at Michigan did not forget 50," he said.

The ploy worked. Mighty OSU struggled with turnovers all afternoon and was upset by the number twelve Wolverines 24–12.

In 1970 it was Woody's turn. Beginning in spring practice, Hayes had his players walk over a rug to get into the locker room. The rug simply had a score on it: 24–12. The players, especially the seniors who had endured the biggest ups and downs of their career versus Michigan, were ready.

The fans were ready, too.

"That stadium was 90 percent full more than an hour before the game," quarterback Rex Kern recalled.

Woody, of course, also was ready. When pulled aside on live televi-

Woody Hayes (right) and Bo Schembechler shake hands during their Ten Year War. (Brockway Sports Photos)

sion before the game by ABC's Chris Schenkel, Hayes responded to a question about Schembechler by saying, "I didn't like the son of a bitch when he played for me, I didn't like the son of a bitch when he coached for me, and I certainly don't like him now."

But those on the inside knew nothing was further from the truth.

"He used to say, 'It's easy to hate Bo when he's not around,' " said OSU All-American lineman John Hicks. "That kind of sums it up."

In what is remembered as one of the most emotional afternoons ever in Ohio Stadium, the Buckeyes did pay back UM with a 20–9 win.

The following year, the revenge game continued, and number three Michigan held on for a 10–7 win. During the game Hayes went into a rage and even shredded a pair of sideline markers in protest of a play in which he thought pass interference should have been called. Rumors swirled that the outburst might lead to his firing, but Michigan's president, AD Don Canham, and Schembechler all went to bat for Hayes both publicly and behind the scenes. They knew Hayes only added to the conference and what was a classic rivalry.

In 1972 Michigan again entered The Game number three in the country, but ninth-ranked Ohio State, led by freshman running back Archie Griffin, held on to win a 14–11 slugfest in the Horseshoe despite being outplayed by UM.

As the Buckeyes assembled in the locker room before the game for words of wisdom from Hayes, they eventually realized their coach was outside waiting for the Michigan bus to arrive, a sight that always stoked the fires inside.

"I didn't believe the sons of Bs would even show up but they did," Hayes told his team.

"To me the 1972 game set the tone for that series," said Hicks, a participant in 1970, 1972, and 1973. "Both teams knew from then on that every game was going to be war."

The next year was even tighter. The teams came in undefeated and played to a 10–10 tie. OSU won extremely intense battles in 1974 and 1975, with both teams ranked in the top five. Michigan won the next three, keeping the Buckeyes out of the end zone each time.

Hayes and Schembechler always had deep respect for each other, but the rivalry took its toll over time. "For the ten years that we had the War we did not speak—ever," Schembechler said recently. "He didn't call me on the phone. When I used to warm up to go out and play Ohio State, he would tell one of my assistants, 'Would you please tell Coach Schembechler I'm ready to meet him at the 50-yard line.' So I'd get to the 50-yard and make sure I didn't cross it."

Woody was fired immediately following the 1978 season after punching Clemson linebacker Charlie Bauman from the sideline during the Gator Bowl, although some in Columbus still contend the axe wouldn't have fallen if he hadn't lost three straight times to Michigan. Soon afterward, some former players decided to organize a special banquet for their beloved Woody. Only people who played or coached for Hayes at Ohio State were invited. No wives. No sports information. No media. No alumni.

"To this day, it was the greatest banquet I ever attended," Schembechler said.

And there are Michiganders living all over Ohio. It's possible just about everybody in Ohio lives near, is related to, or works with someone from Michigan.

There are towns like Toledo and various parts of northeast Ohio that seem evenly flooded with Ohio State and Michigan fans. Gene Fekete, who starred for OSU in 1942 and went on to become an assistant coach at his alma mater, knew there were bragging rights on the line even before he got to participate in The Game. Fekete played high school football in the late 1930s in Findlay, Ohio, which, at the time was home to the Ohio Oil Company. A lot of the people in town associated with Ohio Oil ironically were supporters of Michigan because of ties to the state up north.

"There were people who would remind you whenever they could that they were from Michigan," Fekete said.

Ohio State–Michigan often is described by both sides as the cleanest, hardest-hitting, most emotional game of the season by far. But make no mistake, there isn't any love between the two.

"This is America," former OSU All-American John Hicks said. "We like competition. And in competition you have to have a rival."

And in great competition, you get great and memorable moments. Even casual fans can recall particular moments in the series.

One of the goofier ones came in 1983, when OSU coach Earle Bruce, a disciple of the close-to-the-vest Woody Hayes, called a very unusual play at a crucial moment—Lachey Right. Unfortunately for Ohio State, it's now also known as "the old fumblerooski."

Trailing 17–14 but driving for the winning score, the Buckeyes tried to execute a trick play that had worked to perfection repeatedly in practice. Center Joe Dooley snapped the

The trenches are no place for the meek when Ohio State takes on Michigan. (Jeff Brehm)

ball to Mike Tomczak, who put it on the ground. A pulling Jim Lachey, OSU's star offensive guard, was to pick the ball up and fool the defense. He never got the chance. Dooley kicked the ball trying to block Mike Hammerstein, who eventually recovered the loose pigskin.

Lachey Right now lives in infamy with Desmond Howard's Heisman pose, Rex Kern's interception fest, and other fiascos in Ann Arbor. But Lachey was still glad to see his coach take the risk. "I think that's good. You've got to take some chances in a big game like that," he said.

John Cooper was ostracized for his conservative approach when coaching against Michigan, but in 1998, amidst bitter disappointment over a previous loss to Michigan State, Cooper told offensive coordinator Mike Jacobs to call the plays he wanted.

"He decided to open it up," Jacobs said, "which is always the way I wanted to win the game anyway—to be balanced and not be afraid to throw it and do some things. In order to have that you had to let it hang out."

OSU won going away, 31–16.

But dominating The Game is not a very common feat. Typically both teams are near equals, both are playing for much, and each has scouted the other out, watching weeks and weeks of film. "It wasn't hard at all to prepare for that game," said OSU linebacker Glen Cobb (1979–82). "You knew all week what they were going to do. It was just a matter of execution by Saturday because everyone was up [for the game] all week."

OSU administrator Bill Myles, who served as an assistant to both Hayes and Bruce, said slow and steady was the mantra with both. "With Woody we were playing not to lose," he said. "We didn't beat Michigan and Michigan didn't beat us. We were waiting on them to make a mistake and they were waiting on us. That was the Michigan game."

Although victory brings the highest highs, defeat brings, well, the opposite. Cooper used to say that in football "one week you're sipping the wine, the next you're stomping the grapes." If you insert "year" for "week," you have the Ohio State–Michigan game. The thought of those other guys ruining your season is the only motivation necessary.

Chris Spielman had twenty-nine tackles—a school record—against UM in 1986. When the Buckeyes were nipped 26–24 he was inconsolable. He had played maybe the best game of his life, but it didn't cross his mind.

Even the great Archie Griffin, long considered OSU's most gracious player, said beating the Blue was the best. "The thing I'm most proud of about my college career is that I played on four teams that never lost to Michigan," he said.

Quarterback Cornelius Greene played with Archie from 1972–75 and also shares that 3–0–1 record. He may have logged the best game of his career in Ann Arbor in 1975. Before leading the Buckeyes on a game-tying touchdown march, he made the other ten on the offense pray with him in the huddle.

With the score 14–14, Ray Griffin, Archie's brother, made a crucial interception and OSU punched in the winning score. When the gun sounded, Greene knelt down and wept tears of joy.

He fought nausea in later years when the outcome was the opposite. "I never could take it when we lost to them after I played," he said. "Their fight song even does something to me. It gets in my bones and makes them ache."

Bruce had another feeling in the pit of his stomach when he was fired the Monday of Michigan week in 1987 and the Ohio State Marching Band honored him by performing songs on his front lawn. But Bruce got to taste the fruits of victory a last time upending Michigan in Ann Arbor. He showed the depth of coaching emotion with his memorable fist-pumping celebration.

After that scene Earle went into Michigan's locker room and Coach Bo Schembechler's office to seek out the man who had been such a good friend and combatant. "It's always hard to lose, but I didn't mind it as much today because of all you've been through," Schembechler told Bruce.

Bruce knew what kind of gesture that was, because Bo wanted to beat OSU's brains in every year.

OSU's Top Ten Wins over Michigan

1. **1968 (50–14)**—Coach Woody Hayes often said this was his greatest win, and it came in the form of a blowout of the fourth-ranked Wolverines. OSU goes on to be undisputed national champs.

2. **1954 (21–7)**—Another thrilling home win, another date in the Rose Bowl, and a national championship. OSU broke open a 7–7 game in the final period behind the heroics of halfback Hopalong Cassady and a vaunted defense that made an epic goal-line stand.

3. **2002 (14–9)**—The Buckeyes completed a 13–0 regular season in much the same fashion they did in several league games throughout the season—with clutch fourth-quarter play. Injured tailback Maurice Clarett played on guts and set up the winning touchdown. Fans celebrated OSU's first-ever berth in the BCS title game.

4. **1970 (20–9)**—Both teams came in unbeaten and untied for the first time ever. The Super Sophs avenged their only league loss in three years, a disheartening 24–12 setback in Ann Arbor the year before that cost OSU a repeat national championship.

5. **1975 (21–14)**—The top-ranked Buckeyes turned defeat into victory with two late scores, the latter set up by a key interception by defensive back Ray Griffin. The win kept an undefeated season alive and earned a fourth straight trip to the Rose Bowl.

6. **1979 (18–15)**—OSU was in danger of losing grip on an unbeaten season, Rose Bowl berth, and number one ranking until Jim Laughlin blocked a UM punt late in the game and Todd Bell raced to the end zone with the bounding football for one of the program's biggest road wins ever.

7. **1942 (21–7)**—The Buckeyes continued a late-season surge by burning fourth-ranked Michigan on three scoring pass plays. Soon after, the school had its first national championship.

8. **1955 (17–0)**—Unable to go "bowling" because of the no-repeat rule, the Buckeyes took it out on Michigan. In wrapping up a second straight Big Ten title, the Buckeyes allowed number six UM to cross midfield just once all day.

9. **1961 (50–20)**—Bob Ferguson ran for four scores as OSU ended its season with a blowout. School administrators voted to decline a bid to the Rose Bowl despite the Buckeyes' biggest win at Michigan post–World War II.

10. **1984 (21–6)**—This win earned Ohio State its only out-right Big Ten title of the 1980s and sent Keith Byars, Cris Carter, Pepper Johnson, Chris Spielman, and company to the second of two Rose Bowls of the Earle Bruce era.

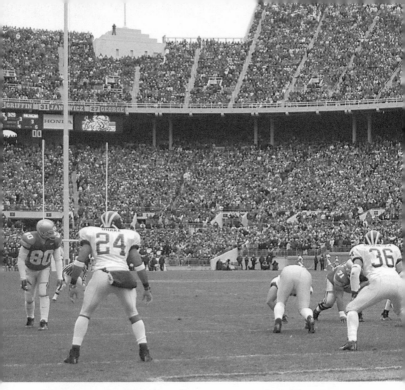

The 2002 version of The Game only added to the magnitude of the rivalry. (Jeff Brehm)

Bruce left Ohio State able to say he had a winning record against the Wolverines (5–4). "I was with a guy who was 16–11–1 against them. That's pretty good, too," he said in reference to the late, great Woody Hayes. "He taught me The Game is important, The Game is the thing, and that you work like hell to beat them."

Some have suggested that the stress put on beating Michigan can be too much, however, especially because Michigan keeps a more low-profile approach about the rivalry during the season.

After all, the entire week is a circus, and every tradition within the program is exhausted from Senior Tackle to the Gold Pants to the Friday night pep rally to the Skull Session. But the players say they enjoy the peripheral attractions of the week so long as they don't distract from the main event.

"I think it's the game itself," Lachey said. "You can talk about all this stuff that's going to happen before and after and all the traditions that are associated with it, but for me the greatest part was getting a chance to line up against them.

"It's a sense of pride. You can finish 9–3, but if you beat Michigan and win your bowl game people forget about those three losses. And if you're [coming in] 12–0 and don't win people are going to say, 'Well, what the hell did you do against Michigan?'

"That's the way it is, and that's the way rivalry games should be."

Added Lachey's Hall of Fame coach, Earle Bruce, "Sometimes people say it is the only game. I don't believe that because you've got to play ten or eleven others, but it is doggoned important. It lets you walk the main streets of Columbus, Ohio. If you lose, you go to the alleys, buddy."

One Small Step for Doss, One Giant Leap for OSU

They say that all championships require sacrifice. In the case of the 2002 Ohio State Buckeyes, that sacrifice often was restraint.

Whether it was the team's field general electing not to chuck one downfield and taking a shot from a linebacker instead, or the willingness of young talent to either switch positions or merely mix in and keep their complaints zipped, or the example of a head coach who worked about eighteen hours a day yet always stressed composure, the Buckeyes were willing to pay the price to be great.

They say all championships require skill. Ohio State usually has that, and in 2002 it had it in spades: a deep, ferocious defensive line with nearly unblockable end Will Smith; a stalwart middle linebacker to feature in the 4–3 defense, Matt Wilhelm, who was capable of playing up to the bar set by predecessors such as Randy Gradishar, Marcus Marek, and Chris Spielman; a secondary that featured standout safety Michael Doss and an unforeseen defensive star in cornerback Chris Gamble; an embarrassment of riches at running back, especially with freshman force Maurice Clarett; an artful group of

Michael Doss (2), here getting an assist from A. J. Hawk (47), stood tall throughout his senior season. (Jeff Brehm)

wideouts headlined by 6'5" Michael Jenkins; a steely signal caller in Craig Krenzel; unspectacular but steady troops at offensive line, fullback, and tight end; and two of the best in the business in the specialty game in placekicker Mike Nugent and punter Andy Groom.

There was speed and toughness everywhere and in some areas impressive depth. That combined with a schedule that included home tilts with rivals Penn State and Michigan had many predicting better things for an OSU squad coming off a 7–5 mark in Coach Tressel's inaugural season.

They say all championships require great leadership. Once a squirrelly team member, Michael Doss became the epitome of a strong leader in his senior season. He was joined in that role by cocaptain Donnie Nickey, a four-year starter at safety, three next to Doss. On offense Krenzel proved to be the ultimate steadying influence, while Clarett, an outspoken freshman, was effective at energizing his offensive line. Even though Clarett sometimes stole the spotlight with public bickering, and despite the fact the team had just thirteen seniors, there were plenty of players who did all the right things on the field and said all the right things off it.

They say all championships require good fortune, never more true than in college football. In 2002 the Buckeyes shook off all the "couldas" and "shouldas" of three decades and manufactured their own luck, often at the make-or-break moments of games. The most dramatic of these came under bleak circumstances at Purdue and in the Fiesta Bowl.

They (whoever "they" are) also say all championships begin in the off-season, but forgive us poor followers of the program if we didn't sense greatness back in April 2002.

What I do remember about that time of year is getting to do a one-on-one interview with Doss for a national magazine.

The undersized but rugged strong safety was an easy choice to be on the publication's regional cover. He was a two-time All-American who had decided while at the lectern and faced with cameras and microphones that he would return for his senior season instead of jumping to the pros. That heartfelt address on January 9, 2002, opened the doors to Doss's personal life, and I found out more about that during my lengthy chat with him at the outset of spring practice in April.

His parents, Gene and Diane Doss, divorced when Mike was a toddler. For a while Mike and his younger sister lived with Diane in Cleveland, but his mom feared that the rough inner city was too dangerous for them. Mike lived with his grandmother, Clara, but after she died of cancer at age forty-six, he was moved from place to place. When he was only seven years old, Mike decided he wanted to live with his uncle Larry in Canton. He was so intent he left elementary school one day and made the 10-mile walk to his uncle's house.

Through it all Mike remained close to his mother, which is exactly why he broke down at the January press conference. He was tempted to jump to the NFL but knew Diane wanted him to finish his education.

Doss always was a stand-up guy on the football field. Listed at a generous 5'11" and 204 pounds, he hit like a runaway train. There was no play Doss didn't intend to make, and he often made good on his intentions.

Off the field Mike was somewhat aloof and leery of the media, although he would at least face the music.

But the commitment to return to OSU made Doss a changed man. In the interview I found him more at ease than I had ever seen him. He was actually enjoying talking with me. All I could think was this was the guy who once had a tape recorder rolling in the inside pocket of his jacket because he was fearful of being misquoted.

Doss reminded me he had won a championship on every level he'd played at since he was eight years old, including a pair of state titles at Canton McKinley High School. "I didn't want that to end," he said. "That's why I came back for my senior year—to have a chance at a championship."

Doss had dreamy but specific bowl scenarios in his head. The one he kept bringing up with me was playing Miami for the national championship. That's all well and good, I thought, but not bloody likely. How wrong I was.

Twelve Up, Twelve Down

Early in the 2002 season, several things about the Buckeyes became clear: They had a real star in the making in Clarett, like Doss a strong-willed performer from northeast Ohio; Krenzel was every bit as heady and reliable at quarterback as his predecessor and former roommate, Steve Bellisari, was maddeningly inconsistent from 1999–2001; the kicking game was outstanding; the defense was tough as nails, especially against the run; and Tressel had no interest in winning any style points, only games.

In the opener with Texas Tech, Clarett became that rare athlete who lives up to his precollege hype in his debut. The former "Mr. Football" award winner in Ohio as well as the *USA Today* prep offensive player of the year, Clarett ripped the Red Raiders for 175 yards and three touchdowns in a 45–21 rout in the Pigskin Classic. He had the OSU sports information department scrambling to see if a freshman had ever started at tailback in his first game, let alone threatened Archie Griffin's first-year rushing record.

Maurice Clarett was a difference-maker in his freshman season of 2002.
(Jeff Brehm)

The second contest of the season wasn't much of one as OSU blasted Kent 51–17. Doss helped set the tone early with a 45-yard interception return for a touchdown. The Golden Flashes didn't cross midfield until late in the second quarter with the Buckeyes enjoying a 38–0 lead.

In game three the defense continued to shine, bottling up quarterback Jason Guesser and eventual Pac-10 champion Washington State in a 25–7 blowout. How much did the Buckeyes try to control the line of scrimmage and the clock? Tressel called for just ten pass plays, with Krenzel completing a mere four. It didn't matter, though, as Clarett took thirty-one handoffs and amassed 230 yards rushing, 9 short of Griffin's freshman record. Griffin was on the sideline late in the game and told Tressel that Clarett had a shot at the mark. Tressel, though, pulled his wunderkind when the defeat of the tenth-ranked Cougars was sure.

Still, praise began to flood in for Clarett, who was being referred to as a Heisman Trophy candidate.

"When I look at him play I see that he's got great eyes," said former OSU power rusher Jim Otis. "He does not make a mistake when cutting and going to the lane. He is just the best at that. He's very patient, he's got good feet and vision, and he's very powerful. He's quick when he needs to be quick. There are not too many anyplace as good as he is."

Tressel's first-ever commitment at OSU, Clarett showed his future focus by graduating early from high school with his sights set on enrolling in time for spring practice. The tactic worked like a charm as he beat out speedy sophomores Lydell Ross and Maurice Hall for the job.

"We knew his passion to achieve was extraordinary," Tressel said. "He knew they weren't all going to be easy adjustments, so he wanted to get some of them out of the way in those first months so that when August hit he would be further along. I think in the back of his mind he felt he wouldn't start as a freshman if he got here in August, and he wanted to be the starter as a freshman. That was his goal."

Just when Clarett had things cooking, he underwent arthroscopic surgery on his right knee to repair some loose cartilage and was ruled out of the next game, a very rare in-state trip to Cincinnati. With the largest crowd ever assembled for a sporting event in Cincinnati on hand, the Bearcats nearly took full advantage and for much of the day they outplayed the visitors. They even had their hands on two different potential game-winning touchdown passes before the Buckeyes held on for a heart-stopping 23–19 win.

In the near disaster the Buckeyes found out a little more about themselves. First, they discovered the margin for error wasn't nearly as great as they first thought. Second, they found that Krenzel was one tough hombre. He shook off a Bellisari-like first half and rallied the Buckeyes with a gritty, twisting touchdown run to the pylon that provided the final points. Third, they found a key piece to the championship puzzle by experimenting with Gamble at cornerback. A wide receiver by trade, the sophomore from Sunrise, Florida, cast a ray of light on OSU's problems in the secondary by making a key interception on his first defensive snap. It would be an omen of things to come.

The Big Ten season brought more potential pitfalls and more dramatic, clutch victories. First the Buckeyes whacked Indiana 45–17, got by Northwestern 27–16, and annihilated San Jose State 50–7 out of conference.

Standing 7–0, which many predicted for them, the Buckeyes faced a game at Wisconsin's ever-challenging Camp Randall Stadium. Camp Randall leads the league in strangely officiated games, drunken students, and launched projectiles—such as marshmallows with coins in them. Surviving there is like waving hello to Nero from the Colosseum floor after he's released the lions.

But that's exactly what OSU did mostly because of the big-play ability of Jenkins, like Gamble a native of Florida. Jenkins took a quick-hitter from Krenzel 47 yards for a score a minute and a half into the game and set up the game-winning TD with a 45-yard grab as the Buckeyes faced third and 6 on their own 16 yard line. Gamble also made a key interception.

The next week OSU was back to the cushy confines of Ohio Stadium against Penn State, but the signs were not good. Clarett suffered a shoulder injury and his counterpart, Penn State running back Larry Johnson, staked the Lions to a 7–0 lead with a nifty first-quarter TD scamper. Sensing a monumental

Matt Wilhelm (35) and Robert Reynolds (44) bottle up Penn State running back Larry Johnson. (Jeff Brehm)

struggle, defensive coordinator Mark Dantonio put his troops on the attack all day. It paid off in a big way when Gamble—who opened at both wideout and corner to become OSU's first two-way starter in three decades—intercepted a Zack Mills pass at the PSU 40 and zigged and zagged his way to Ohio State's only touchdown of the day.

Mike Nugent later added his second field goal and the defense pitched a second-half shutout in the 13–7 win. The Buckeyes sang "Carmen Ohio" and sprinted to the locker room, another pothole in the championship road avoided.

That's when another trend emerged: These Buckeyes were downright stingy in the second half. They'd kept Wisconsin off the board in the third and fourth quarters until they could figure out a way to win and did the same thing to Joe Paterno's befuddled Lions.

When asked how his team made such wonderful adjustments during games, Tressel quipped, "Well, there's a school of thought that we do a poor job all week." He also praised his coaches for scouting and players for doing their homework.

"Our players recognize those things, they talk about them on the sideline, they do a good job of communication with the coaches," he said. "Our coaches are good listeners, and I think that's very important in terms of making adjustments. The coaches don't pretend that they have all the answers, because the guys are in the arena."

That trust, combined with OSU's penchant for pulling out tight contests, began to build upon itself to a point that the players had total belief in Tressel's tactics. "Every aspect of the game of football, of college football, he wants to do things right," Wilhelm said of Tressel. "And he wants to do things right not only as a head coach for his coaching staff but for us as players. We've just got total confidence in our coaches that the game plan is going to be pretty precise, and that if we go out and execute we're going to win the ballgame."

"All that stuff he preaches is great," added Kirk Herbstreit, a former Buckeye now known more as an ESPN analyst, "but the way you really make the kids buy into it is win. By avoiding a loss to Cincinnati, it started to grow. Then, you're in trouble against Penn State but you pull that one out. When you find ways to win when the ball can bounce either way, it does a lot for the confidence of a team."

The animal grew some more in one of the most memorable Columbus Novembers in years.

On November 2, the Buckeyes dumped a ranked Minnesota squad, 34–3. As an added bonus fans were informed of several upsets around the country, including Notre Dame's fall from the ranks of the unbeaten in a 14–7 loss to Boston College.

On November 9, OSU sprinkled some more pixie dust in a 10–6 triumph at Purdue. In West Lafayette the defense allowed only a field goal in the second half, but it appeared for a while to be the difference in the game. Trailing 6–3 with less than two minutes to go and staring at fourth and 1 — make that fourth and championship — the Buckeyes ran a play for the ages.

With the blessing of the coaches, Krenzel called for a pass that was designed to free up tight end Ben Hartsock underneath a streaking Jenkins. But under duress Krenzel only had time to step up and loft one for big number 12. Jenkins ran right under the aerial and secured it for an unlikely touchdown with 1:36 to play. Gamble's acrobatic interception near midfield moments later preserved the win.

On the jubilant trip home, OSU got word of Oklahoma's 30–26 loss at Texas A&M, which appeared to put the Buckeyes in the driver's seat for the Fiesta Bowl.

"Mike Doss was on his cell phone with someone who was kind of giving us play-by-play," Wilhelm said. "I'm sure knowing Mike it was Brent Musburger or somebody like that. Obviously, after the interception late in the game we knew that they had lost and that we'd be moving up. It's a wonderful thing to control your own destiny."

Destiny is exactly what the Buckeyes had on their minds as they endured another extreme test at Illinois on November 16. Playing without Clarett for the second time in three weeks, OSU found itself offensively challenged once again. Meanwhile, the defending Big Ten champion Illini, losing record be damned, were putting together a season's-best effort. The teams were tied after three quarters and then four after UI's John Gockman drilled a 48-yard field goal at the end of regulation, forcing the Buckeyes to play an extra session for the first time in school history. It would serve as the perfect precursor to the BCS title game.

Krenzel kept things going in the overtime by picking up a first down with his feet on third and long. That was followed by an 8-yard TD jaunt by Hall, OSU's leading rusher with Clarett on the sideline. Just like at Cincinnati, Illinois had its hands on a TD pass in the final moments but officials correctly ruled Walter Young bobbled it in the end zone.

The Buckeyes were 12–0 for the first time in school history but there were two rocky mountains yet to climb: a home date with hated rival Michigan and the bowl game.

Going Out in Style

You could understand if a Buckeye fan watched the Michigan game through his own fingers. After all, in the John Cooper era alone there was enough heartache at the hands of Maize and Blue to fill one of those 3-inch-thick paperback novels.

Undefeated seasons went kaput in the regular-season finale in 1993, 1995, and 1996. OSU could have returned the favor in 1997 but made one too many blunders. And then there were embarrassments in Michigan Stadium in 1989 and 1991.

But whether it was the fact that the Buckeyes had lifted some of the hex in Ann Arbor the year before or actually had managed to find a calm inner strength with the entire city in a frenzy, I was shocked to see a group so loose before a game some were labeling the biggest ever played in the Horseshoe.

"The week leading up to the game is a little more emotional, especially when there are big things on the line," said Krenzel, ironically the only Michigan native on the OSU roster, "but once you step out on the field and the game begins it's just another football game. They're going to play us tougher than anyone's played us all year. We know that. We know we have to play better than we have all year."

Tressel also showed he still had his sense of humor when reporters assumed the workaholic coach would burn even more midnight oil for Michigan. "We're about out of oil," said Tressel, promising he would actually get a few hours sleep during the week.

Admitting the importance of The Game while allowing his players to still be themselves was Tressel's intent all along, just as it had been in his first encounter with Michigan, a 26–20 win in Ann Arbor in 2001. It was an approach that was almost a complete turnaround from Cooper, who used to downplay the contest publicly while preventing his players from doing interviews and taking part in just about every other normal activity during the week.

Wilhelm, who played for both men, wasn't afraid to say what the fans and media were—a loss to Michigan would have ruined everything again. "It may not be fair but it comes with

Ohio State's Three-Time Football All-Americans

Chic Harley, running back (1916–17, 1919)
Wesley Fesler, end (1928–30)
Lew Hinchman, halfback (1930–32)
Merle Wendt, end (1934–36)
Archie Griffin, tailback (1973–75)
Tom Skladany, punter (1974–76)
Michael Doss, safety (2000–02)

the territory," said the senior middle linebacker. "We schedule Michigan at the end of the year for a reason."

Not surprisingly, the player embracing Michigan week the most was Doss.

The Monday before The Game, Doss admitted he already couldn't sleep, but not because of visions of the Fiesta Bowl, Senior Day, or anything other than one word: *Michigan*.

"When you see that maize and blue come out of that locker room, that's the number one motivation right there regardless of everything extra that's riding on that," he said. "I remember realizing that my freshman year. When that maize and blue comes out of that locker room you've got to be ready to play no matter what the records are."

Doss was so intense leading into the week that a reporter asked him if he was even able to enjoy his senior season with all the pressure mounting.

"I started enjoying it when camp came," he said. "I remember telling a couple of you guys how we'd be, but there were a lot of predictions out there of 10–3, 11–2 at best. But I envisioned good things for us a long time ago. I kind of willed into my desire to be a winner. I've done that since I was a little kid. So being 12–0 right now doesn't surprise me. It's something I thought about years ago. Now it's here and I'm taking it in stride.

"This is what you dream about. This is what you're here for."

Doss had an emotional beginning to 2002, and thanks to a stellar senior season, he had an emotional swan song in Ohio Stadium, as well.

He was visibly moved to be announced with the seniors moments before the November 23 game, and as fate would have it, his dream of playing in the national championship game was almost a reality as he went back to defend against a Michigan game-winning pass attempt with one second left.

Nickel back Will Allen was on the field, too, and Doss had just told him, "Don't do anything too crazy." Allen didn't. He simply read the play, realized UM quarterback John Navarre was dialed into Braylon Edwards, stepped up at the goal line, and intercepted the ball—right in front of Gamble and Doss. Pandemonium ensued as many in the record crowd stormed the field.

Ohio State 14, Michigan 9.

At the end of games, Doss was known to walk to midfield, take a knee, and give a prayer of thanks. This time he sprinted, and when he knelt down with chaos and fan euphoria all around him, he wept. He had met his ultimate goal in his final home game as a Buckeye and his family was there to see it.

Just as the Buckeyes had bucked a painful trend by beating Michigan with all the chips on the table, followers of the program figured it was time to go ahead and get rid of a thirty-four-year drought between national championships.

"It's time to put the '68 team to rest," said former Buckeye and Columbus businessman Larry Zelina, who helped the 1968 team to the title and watched so many teams fail thereafter. "There have been two or three other teams of ours that should have done it. Ohio State deserves to be at its rightful place atop college football. Sometimes it makes me sad that we're the most recent reference point."

Otis, a junior on that great 1968 team, agreed. "If they can do it, it takes us off the hook," he said. "They've been talking about us too long."

Amazingly, at 13–0 and with a season full of clutch and unselfish play, the Buckeyes were given no chance. That's because as the number two team in the final BCS standings they drew a date in the Fiesta Bowl with defending national champion Miami (Florida), proud owners of a thirty-four-game winning streak. The Hurricanes had a pair of Heisman Trophy finalists in quarterback Ken Dorsey and tailback Willis McGahee, a stingy offensive line, qualified stars at wideout (Andre Johnson) and tight end (Kellen Winslow Jr.), and a nasty defense with players who could run like deer.

Analysts said Miami's experience, thirst for greatness, and superior skill would be too much for any team to overcome, let alone an unspectacular, thick-legged one from the Midwest. Oddsmakers installed OSU as much as a two-touchdown underdog. Some predicted worse.

Orlando Sentinel columnist Mike Bianchi seemed to sum up the feelings of Floridians, fans of wide-open football, and skeptics by writing before the game that OSU fans had descended on the Arizona desert only to see the carnage ahead.

"These simple, poor, plodding people are getting ready to step into another realm beyond their comprehension," he wrote. "The Buckeyes aren't going to come within three touchdowns of winning this game. Not with a quarterback who couldn't start for any of the five Division 1-A teams in the state of Florida. The Buckeyes, bless their boring little Big Ten hearts, couldn't throw change into a tollbooth receptacle.

"Ohio State will find out that their old-school ways simply won't work against a program that wrote the book on new-age football."

You can imagine Bianchi's smirk when Miami took a 7–0 lead on a Dorsey TD pass to Roscoe Parrish, who beat the isolated Doss on the play. You can also imagine Bianchi's disbelief as OSU dominated the second quarter with a defensive surge ignited by a Doss interception. With Dorsey on his back foot dealing with pressure he hadn't seen all year and Krenzel foiling Miami's push with crucial runs, OSU built up a 17–7

Momentum swung OSU's way in the BCS title game when Darrion Scott (56) pounced on a fumble by Miami quarterback Ken Dorsey.
(Jeff Brehm)

lead. McGahee tightened the score to 17–14 with a fourth-quarter TD run, and just as at Illinois, the game was extended to overtime on a last-second field goal.

How appropriate. Undefeated and playing the nation's top team toe to toe, the Buckeyes still needed one last batch of karma, one last unforgettable sequence of plays to claim the trophy.

At the coaches dinner, the first event of the week, president of the Fiesta Bowl John Junker greeted Tressel and Miami's Coach Larry Coker by saying, "Gee, wouldn't it be great if we have a double-overtime game?"

The Buckeyes completed that dream with a 31–24 win in two OTs. To do it they picked up a fourth and 14, drew a game-saving penalty in the end zone on another fourth down in the first session, then took the lead on a Clarett TD and held on for dear life in the second.

Pandemonium again.

Greats such as Eddie George, Shawn Springs, David Boston, and Raymont Harris stood on the sideline when Dorsey's final fling alighted on the Sun Devil Stadium grass—guys who have played in huge college games and in the case of George, the Super Bowl. They were nervous wrecks until that clinching moment.

Rex Kern, who piloted OSU's last title some thirty-four years earlier, was as giddy as, well, a college student. He lied to get by security by saying he was a member of Krenzel's family just so he could congratulate the heady QB. It was a priceless moment as the two beamed side by side, looking very much like father and son.

Expressions of joy abounded, whether they were from fans, players, coaches, or administrators after what was being termed the greatest college game ever. "I tell you, during the season, maybe it's just because I'm getting older, but there were a lot of very emotional moments for me this year," said Archie Griffin, now an associate athletic director. "To beat Michigan, to beat Purdue and Illinois the way we did, that got to me. After the Purdue game I just felt in my mind that we would be playing in the national championship game because I thought, 'These guys won't lose; they just will not lose.'

"They set the goal, did everything possible, didn't let anything get in their way, and got it done."

Krenzel, the game's MVP, and Doss, the defensive MVP, shared the spotlight in the on-field postgame celebration. Back in the quiet of the hotel room hours later, Doss got to savor the moment with Tressel, who told Doss three games into the 2001 season after a loss at UCLA, "I'm not going to let you

Head coach Jim Tressel and seniors Donnie Nickey (25) and Kenny Peterson (97) celebrate the national title. (Jeff Brehm)

Ballad of the Buckeyes

(A poem written to commemorate the 2002 national championship team by Professor of English David Citino, poet laureate for the university)

> *From the banks of the Olentangy*
> *they came, to show the world Ohio's here.*
> *They made the whirling winds shout O,*
> *and the desert bloomed scarlet and gray.*
> *To the roll of those old heroes, add*
> *these newer names, whose deeds become*
> *our breathless, mortal lore. It's nothing*
> *but a game, some people claim. Yes, and so*
> *much more. Laboring, these athletes*
> *proved to each and all, especially themselves,*
> *what miracles can be achieved*
> *when young ones come, as one, to learn*
> *from those who've learned before,*
> *to compose on lined and numbered fields,*
> *in classrooms, labs, and dorms, a season*
> *of perfection, a symphony of champions.*

Note: Citino was asked by OSU's new president Karen Holbrook to write a poem from the university point of view on the football team's national title. A longtime Buckeye fan, he accepted gladly.

"I put it in the form of a ballad, and I thought of the old English and Scottish and Irish ballads where the troubadour tells the story of great deeds and heroic actions of the past, because it occurred to me that fifty years from now, a hundred years from now, people will be talking about that game in the same way people now talk about the Snow Bowl against Michigan," he said. "It just becomes a kind of timeless piece of lore.

"So, I wanted to give praise to the great effort of the team and the coaches but I also wanted to put everything in its context. Yes, these players are incredibly gifted and talented, but they're students. Throughout this whole thing they went to class, they went to their labs, and they had to achieve in that way as well."

leave Ohio State University without being the best player you can be," a moment that stuck with the safety.

"He was so excited about the results of the decision he made," Tressel said. "I think he'll even be more and more and more excited as time goes. I think it was a great message to young people in college football and young people that want to stay and finish tasks and get some of the goals that [they] set for [themselves]."

The team returned home to a heroes' welcome, except for a handful of players including Doss, who had to go straight to an all-star game. Finally, OSU fans got to flock into frozen Ohio Stadium on January 18, 2003, more than two weeks after the title was in hand, to show their affection. Temperatures were measured at minus-three with the wind chill, but there was plenty of warmth to pass around.

Michael Doss was asked to say a few words to the crowd as a senior captain. After a short address he turned to his head coach and said, "A year ago we sat in a room and we had a mission. Coach, mission accomplished."

They embraced. The crowd of approximately 52,000 roared. The national championship trophies glistened in the winter sun.

A Century of Great Tradition

T hey can throw as many flaming spears as they want in Tallahassee, play for a hundred Old Oaken Buckets in Indiana, and run around with steers and buffaloes until the cows come home out West, there still can't be a college football program with more tradition—and traditions—than Ohio State.

When you look at the entire life and scope of the program, all the great players who were All-Americans and went on to the NFL, all the outstanding teams that won conference championships and national titles, the hall of fame coaches, the octogenarian stadium, and the nationally renowned band, you see that Ohio State is in very select company. Then, when you factor in the importance of the program and the gameday experience to the community, it's just about impossible to find a match.

But what trumps it all is the amazing number of football-related traditions that have been going on for decades at OSU.

These rituals range from behind-the-scenes habits such as the placing of buckeye leaf stickers on the players' helmets to the pageantry at Ohio Stadium and its latest addendum, the team singing the school alma mater after the game.

"I don't claim to know all about every school's traditions," former Buckeye Kirk Herbstreit said, "but the only school that comes to mind that can rival Ohio State on that is Texas A&M. They've got the twelfth man, they have yell practice on Friday night before the game and like 35,000 people show up for that, they have a different chant for every situation that can come up during a game.

"But even with that I can't imagine any other school that has as many traditions as Ohio State."

Herbstreit has a pretty good perspective on the matter. He has been an analyst for ESPN's *College GameDay* show since before the 1996 season and in that time has covered games and been on the campuses of major programs all over the country.

Longtime OSU assistant coach Esco Sarkkinen used to preach that there were five irrefutable great traditions of Ohio State football: the dotting of the "i" in Script Ohio, the Captains Breakfast, Senior Tackle, the gold pants charms players received for beating Michigan, and All-Americans being honored with a buckeye tree in the Buckeye Grove.

Along with those storied five are so many more, a list that dates back prior to 1900 and seems to grow yearly.

Bill Myles, associate athletic director and former assistant coach of the football team under Woody Hayes and Earle Bruce, became the unofficial keeper of the traditions in place of Sarkkinen, who died in 1998. When asked if he believed there were too many of them, Myles said, "No way. This is the kind of program where all that stuff should be embraced."

Jim Tressel agreed. When he became head coach in 2001, he instituted a few more, requiring players to form an Iowa-like "Hive" of solidarity in the end zone before the game and to sing "Carmen Ohio" after, win or lose. He also made sure to bring the team by the band's Skull Session on the way to Ohio Stadium.

"I thought, 'Man, I was here for three years and coached here and that's supposed to be one of the traditions. How can

A Chilling Group: The Best Damn Band In The Land

Almost since its first recorded game in 1890, the OSU football team has strived to please its fans by being proclaimed the top unit in the country. The OSU Marching Band? It just has to show up.

Originally formed as a military band in 1879, "The Pride of the Buckeyes" developed into one of the nation's most recognizable groups of musicians—a 225-member all-brass band. The university and its alumni have dubbed it "The Best Damn Band In The Land," and no one seems to argue, at least not inside the state's borders.

"I like the fact that our band is so well thought of," former Buckeye great Archie Griffin said. "I look forward to seeing them come down that ramp. I didn't get to see it when I was a player, but when I got to see it as a fan and a spectator then I realized how special it was."

The band performs several traditional songs and formations, the most noteworthy being Script Ohio. "As a fan without a doubt my favorite tradition related to the program is Script Ohio," ex-Buckeye quarterback Kirk Herbstreit said. "And when they make their entrance from the ramp, I want to cover the kickoff I get so fired up."

The Ramp Entrance, which began in 1928, is a continuation of a long pregame agenda that begins with the Skull Session, which eventually developed into a free concert/pep rally featuring the band in St. John Arena. After prepping for the on-field show one last time at the Skull Session, the band marches south in ranks of twelve to drum cadence across Woody Hayes Drive to Ohio Stadium.

The dramatic entrance includes a back bend by the drum major at the front of the ranks, who touches his plume to the ground, raises up, and leads a forward storm toward the South Stands to "Buckeye Battle Cry," one of the school's two fight songs.

The band has aided many of the most moving moments at Ohio State. When it played on Earle Bruce's front lawn as a show of support for the fired head coach, Bruce bawled. So did the crowd in Ohio Stadium when it played during a ceremony for Woody Hayes after his death.

The Ohio State Marching Band consistently stirs emotions on game day.
(Jeff Brehm)

I not see that?' " he explained. "So we were talking as a staff one time and I said, 'What do you think about our guys experiencing that?' That way when they left they could not only say it was one of the traditions, they could have been a part of it.

"Also it lets those people know who live and die Ohio State and love 'The Best Damn Band In The Land' that it was important for us that we appreciate them. I think it's good for both.

"I hope by their total experience it tells them the game isn't just about what it does for me. The game is what it does for all involved."

Tressel's predecessor, John Cooper, was a Southerner who came to OSU from Arizona State. He admitted being blown away by how much Ohio State taps into its history and tradition.

"Most great universities have traditions like that, although Ohio State sure does have a lot of them," he said. "I liked all that stuff. I like the Buckeye Grove, the Gold Pants, 'Carmen Ohio.' You hear about the dotting of the 'i' all over the country, and everyone knows about the buckeye leaves on the helmets. I thought all that stuff was great."

However, one of the oldest and most cherished traditions of all nagged at Cooper most of his time in Columbus: Senior Tackle. The ritual of the team's seniors hitting the blocking sled one last time before The Game with Michigan just about vanished when Cooper tried to low key the event, build it back up amid criticism, and then put it under lock and key when his feeble record versus Michigan became a national statistic.

"It seemed like whatever way I did it, it was wrong," he said. "That got to be something we did with thousands and thousands of fans and was sort of a big show and I don't think it was ever meant to be that way."

Lucky charms, pep rallies, trophies, and rituals, all that stuff is nice to an old warrior like John Hicks but isn't as

Former All-American lineman John Hicks claims Ohio State's greatest tradition is its players. (Brockway Sports Photos)

important as the people playing their heart out for OSU.

"I think our number one tradition is the guys," said Hicks, an award-winning offensive tackle of the early 1970s. "If you want to get into traditions you start with your teammates. When I was in the pros we had guys who wouldn't speak to each other. It was more distant. But the Buckeyes always stuck together. Only Ohio State, Oklahoma, Nebraska, Notre Dame, and Michigan have that kind of camaraderie. *That* is what makes your program special.

"Woody used to say, 'The finest people you'll ever meet are right here in this room,' and, you know, he was right."

What follows is a look at some of Ohio State's more prominent football traditions.

Block "O"

A special section for almost 1,500 students, Block "O" keeps fans involved with cheers and stunts with flash cards throughout the game. It was started in 1938 by cheerleader Clancy Isaac, who stayed involved with it for forty years. It has moved from midfield to a longtime perch in the north end to its current spot in the permanent South Stands.

Brutus Buckeye

OSU's familiar mascot, who resembles the nut of a buckeye tree, was born in 1965 and was helped into prominence by Dave Hocevar, a "Super Soph" who shared Brutus duties with junior Al Kundtz in 1968.

"When we were Brutus, the mascot was kind of evolving," he said. "At first Brutus was just a product of Block 'O.' The Rose Bowl that season was the first time he traveled.

"Those first couple years it just resembled some nut walking around. You could see your shoes and that was about it, so we were pretty much restricted to walking around on the track. The second year I got brave and went out on the field for the coin toss."

Back then, Brutus was a shell 48 inches in diameter with eyes coming up to the chest of the inhabitant. Basically, it looked like a brown medicine ball with legs. In the early 1970s Brutus donned a huge gray cap and had moving eyebrows. Eventually, Brutus's head was reduced and he became a member of the cheerleading squad who performed stunts and also mingled with fans during games.

Brutus Buckeye helps lead the charge. (Jeff Brehm)

Brutus's head was stolen out of the car of Brutus portrayer Eric Mayers in 1984 on the day before the game with Michigan. It was the only head and Mayers was to wear the getup for his last game in Ohio Stadium. A man found it in a trash bin and returned it for $1,500. Every nut has his price.

Buckeye Grove

Buckeye Grove houses one buckeye tree for every All-American football player at Ohio State. It's been shifted from outside Ohio Stadium's east side to the southwest area as part of the recent stadium renovation project. It has a walkway, picnic table, and plaque for every tree.

"That's one the guys really enjoy," Myles said. "It's really important to them. The only thing is they have a hard time finding their tree because there are so many. When Jim Marshall's in town he'll call me and tell me to meet him at his tree so he can show it to somebody."

Buckeye Leaves

The familiar leaves on the helmets, a tradition coach Woody Hayes began in 1968, are actually stickers awarded to the players by the assistant coaches for standout plays in games. The coaches grade the game film on Sunday and hand the list to the equipment staff on Monday.

"Of all the traditions we do, that's probably the most important one," said Jason Eberly, a student who assisted equipment manager Danny Swain during the 2002 national championship season.

Eberly said the most leaves he had to affix for a player in one week was twelve for senior safety Donnie Nickey. Several players nearly filled their helmets in the fourteen-game season. In past years star players such as Art Schlichter, Keith Byars, Chris Spielman, Eddie George, and Antoine Winfield also had almost entirely adorned helmets.

The leaves are passed out more liberally these days than they were originally. In 1968, a year in which the Buckeyes won the national championship, junior defensive halfback Ted

Provost was awarded the most leaves for the season—thirteen.

"Some guys on the team nicknamed him 'Tree,' because of that," Myles said. "They still call him that."

The Captains Breakfast

The Captains Breakfast is another tradition that dates back to the Depression era. The first annual Captains Breakfast took place at Scioto Country Club on December 16, 1934.

"The one that I like is the Captains Breakfast because that thing has been going on for years and years," Archie Griffin said. "You have captains that come back from way back. The fact that all the captains have the opportunity to get together every year, I think it's very, very special."

The former players share stories, brag on their teams, and welcome in the new captains, who receive a pin and silver mug.

The breakfast has been held almost every year during Homecoming weekend. Tressel recently shifted it from the Sunday after Homecoming to the morning of the game.

"Carmen Ohio"

Another Tressel move is having the team sing "Carmen Ohio," the school's alma mater. Linebacker Cie Grant gave the song more notoriety at a celebration of the 2002 national championship team by singing a soulful version of "Carmen" for about 50,000 frozen fans in Ohio Stadium.

Columbus native and OSU student-athlete Fred Cornell began to pen phrases of the song in 1902 on his way back from the football team's painful 86–0 loss at Michigan. The finished product was first published in the *Lantern*, the school newspaper, on October 10, 1906. It has served as a stirring tribute to school pride ever since.

"'Carmen Ohio' has always been one of the songs that gets the best of me emotionally," Herbstreit said. "There's a lot in those words. The song represents different eras in your life."

Carmen Ohio

Oh! Come let's sing Ohio's praise,
And songs to Alma Mater raise;
While our hearts rebounding thrill,
With joy which death alone can still.
Summer's heat or Winter's cold,
The seasons pass, the years will roll;
Time and change will surely show
How firm thy friendship O-HI-O.

Gold Pants

Maybe the most important symbol related to the team, the Gold Pants are awarded to players, coaches, and administrators after each win over Michigan.

On his arrival in 1934, coach Francis Schmidt, aware of tough times in recent years versus OSU's archrival, told his team, "They put their pants on one leg at a time just like you do." As a reminder of Michigan's mortality, gold charms resembling the pants of Michigan players were doled out thereafter. OSU won Schmidt's first five games against the Wolverines by a combined score of 132–0.

Sarkkinen, a star player in the late 1930s and an assistant coach from 1946–77, is believed to have more Gold Pants than anyone—seventeen. The charms have the player's initials inscribed on the back and the final score on the front.

"To see those Gold Pants in your hand is to realize you accomplished one of your goals. It's a symbol of all the hard work you went through," said three-time All-American safety Michael Doss, who gave his first pair to his uncle and his other to his mother.

"When you give your Gold Pants to someone, that's making a tremendous statement," said OSU administrator Bill Myles, who won four pair as an assistant coach to Woody Hayes and Earle Bruce. "One guy told me he told his girlfriend, 'If we ever break up, the only thing I want back is my Gold Pants.' "

"Hang On Sloopy"

A staple of game day, especially at the end of the third quarter, "Sloopy" was adopted by the OSU Marching Band while it was a chart-topping hit by the Ohio-born band The McCoys in 1965. The OSU band first played it—swaying all the way through—on October 9 of that year for a home game with Illinois.

The lyrics of "Sloopy" actually refer to Dorothy Sloop, a New Orleans nightclub musician originally from Steubenville, Ohio, who "lives in a very bad part of town."

"In my head I heard it as a song for a brass band," John Tatgenhorst told Ohio State *Alumni Magazine* in 1996. A music student in 1965, Tatgenhorst pestered band director Charles Spohn to let him arrange it for the band. Spohn, who thought the chords were too basic, finally relented. Tatgenhorst worked on the arrangement for four hours and was paid $20.

"I figured they would use the thing only once or twice anyway," he said.

Wrong. The simple song has had amazing lasting power. In fact a House resolution in 1985 proclaimed "Hang On Sloopy" Ohio's state rock song.

The Illibuck

The trophy that is awarded to the winner of the Ohio State–Illinois game dates back to 1925 when it was a live turtle. It has been a wooden replica ever since 1927. If there is a changeover, the Illibuck is presented to the winner prior to the next game.

"Ohio State won it like fifteen years in a row (1968–82), so for a long time there was no presentation," Myles said. "When Glen Mason came over here [in 1978], he started saying how we have to win the Illibuck because previously he was on the Illinois staff. People didn't know what he was talking about."

The Illibuck became a more prized possession in the 1980s and 1990s when the series was more even. OSU and Illinois, by the way, have met every year since 1914, making it one of the longest-standing rivalries in the country.

Scarlet and Gray

OSU's recognizable colors are unique to all of college football. The three students who in 1878 decided on the colors originally opted for orange and black, but they were told to pick something else when it was determined Princeton already had the same combo. They then chose scarlet and gray because "it was a pleasing combination," according to one committee member.

Script Ohio

Believe it or not, claims that the Michigan band first performed Script Ohio appear to be true. There is documentation of the UM band doing so at an OSU–Michigan game in Ohio Stadium on October 15, 1932.

OSU's Department of Music asked visiting bands to come up with a unique salute to Ohio State that year to help celebrate the ten-year anniversary of the stadium. There is at least one account of Michigan giving the band charts to OSU Band Director Eugene Weigel after the UM band formed "Ohio" in cursive on the field.

However, OSU's familiar march in scriptlike fashion through the four letters appears to be both initiated and perfected by "The Best Damn Band In The Land." All official OSU literature claims the Ohio State Marching Band first performed it at halftime of the Indiana game on October 24, 1936.

The formation is climaxed as a fourth- or fifth-year sousaphone player follows the lead of the drum major by high stepping to a spot that signifies the dotting of the "i." There have been a few honorary dotters of the "i" as well, including Woody Hayes, Bob Hope, Buster Douglas, and the seniors from the 2002 national championship team.

Senior Tackle

Dates have varied as to the beginning of Senior Tackle, but it definitely started when a group of seniors asked head coach John Wilce if they could hit the tackling dummy one last time, likely in 1913. The event has been both private and public in years following but has remained a tribute to the hard work of outgoing players.

"As a player, sentimentally I think Senior Tackle is the best," Herbstreit said. "That one just stands out in your experiences."

Countered Hicks: "I always thought Senior Tackle was kind of depressing."

Superfans

Any great program also has its share of great fans, and the Buckeye Nation is as strong as ever these days. It's also got its share of, ahem, overzealous followers.

You know, like the person who put a bag of Tostitos on Woody Hayes's gravesite and took pictures of it for the Internet to make sure the Old Man knew his beloved Buckeyes were playing for the national title in the Fiesta Bowl.

Every ardent OSU fan, it seems, knows of an even more dedicated one, like Bynum "Trot" Trotter. A longtime administrative assistant in the university's Department of Physical Education, Trotter operated the scoreboards at OSU basketball and football games for forty-seven years. From the time Ohio Stadium opened in 1922 until the 1970s, he missed exactly three football games. Robert E. Bulen, a chief bailiff for the Franklin County Municipal Court who prefers to go by "Buckeye Bob," has attended every OSU game—home, away, and bowl—for the twenty-seven years through the 2003 Fiesta Bowl. "Buckeye Bob" left for Tempe without a ticket, scored one, and ran his string of games to 336 games dating back to October 11, 1975, when OSU beat Iowa in Ohio Stadium.

The list of fanaticos like "Buckeye Bob"—people who never miss a game, tailgate religiously, and soak up every minute of the game-

The fans didn't think so, though. They came out in droves to see it and to hear encouraging words from speakers such as former coaches Hayes and Bruce and ex-players such as Rex Kern and Chris Spielman.

Tunnel of Pride

Devised by athletic director Andy Geiger and Kern and organized by Griffin, the Tunnel of Pride began in 1994 in hopes of turning around a losing streak to Michigan. It worked. After

day experience—would be just as long as an all-time list of former players. It's also quite a varied group. For every intoxicated student and minimum-wage earner with a painted face, there's an esteemed professional with the same passion.

Take Dr. Robert Stevenson, for example. A dentist at the university, Stevenson also is an aficionado of anything related to the football program. He met his wife at OSU and graduated from the dental school in 1975. Their daughter, Jody, was the first female deaf cheerleader at OSU (1998–99). Son Robby, whose full name is Robert Woodrow Stevenson, was born at University Hospital the very night of Woody Hayes's infamous punch at the 1978 Gator Bowl.

A fifty-year follower of the Buckeyes, Dr. Stevenson was never so thrilled as he was after OSU survived Michigan 14–9 in Ohio Stadium to end the 2002 regular season. So thrilled that he jumped down from the stands to the field with a gaggle of students and promptly broke his ankle in two places.

After the thirteenth game of the 113th season of Ohio State football, Stevenson had to be carried away on a stretcher and taken to a hospital, where doctors inserted thirteen screws in his tibia and fibula.

"I took it as a lucky omen," he said.

running onto the field through a "tunnel" of former players and their family members, the Buckeyes dumped the Maize and Blue, 22–6. The next year, the Tunnel shot OSU off to a 45–26 pasting of Notre Dame. Administrators generally plan the Tunnel for one big home game every year.

The Victory Bell

Members of the OSU fraternity Alpha Phi Omega ring the Victory Bell immediately following each home win by the

Buckeyes. The bell was a gift to the university from the class of 1943. The original intention was for the bell to be placed on the Oval in the middle of campus and for it to ring after every athletic victory. Instead it was cast—weighing more than 2,400 pounds—moved to the southeast tower of Ohio Stadium, and used to signify wins on the football field. Up to this time, the bell has been rung after each victory for fifty seasons with one exception: After a 38–0 win over Iowa in 1965, the bell was silenced. A prankster had stolen its sixty-pound clapper and hung it from the William Oxley Thompson statue in front of the main library, ironically on the edge of the Oval where the bell had been intended to rest.

Archie Griffin:
All-American Idol

M y first impressions of Archie Griffin face to face were just as I'd always heard and expected: class, class, class.

One of the all-time great collegiate running backs, the focal point of one of the all-time great eras at Ohio State (1972–75), Archie was always just as impressive in person as he was on the football field. Because of that, as well as his local background and love of the Buckeyes, he is probably the most beloved figure in the history of the program.

After Archie moved up the food chain of the athletic administration at his alma mater, it became a little tougher to get to see him. I drew an assignment one fall of doing a "Michigan memory" with him, having him discuss his recollections from his four games against the Maize and Blue. It was the kind of interview he had granted a thousand times. His secretary set up a midmorning appointment. I had fifteen minutes blocked off.

So I showed up at his St. John Arena office and waited. And waited. And waited. Archie was hung up in a meeting, then a conference call, then an impromptu radio interview. That's when I began to have a sacrilegious feeling: I was a little ticked off at Archie. What was I, a stack of wood just sitting in his waiting room?

Of course I should have known better. When Archie finally emerged he was extremely apologetic. He insisted on taking me to lunch and told me I could have as much time as I needed. We walked across Lane Avenue to get a bite to eat— just as his old coach, Woody Hayes, did on a daily basis—and it took us several minutes just to get to our seats. Everybody had to say hi to Archie. They reached for his hand. They asked him how the football team looked at practice. I felt like I was a Secret Service man walking with the president.

I had seen this scene play out many times before, but always in an athletic setting. For example, Archie always struggles to get from the locker room up to his perch in the press box before football games because he is intercepted by well-wishers and bombarded with autograph and picture requests. It's the same deal at a basketball game, wrestling meet, field hockey game, you name it.

But when I saw Archie in the restaurant with everyone putting down their forks and beverages just to smile at him or, in the case of a couple people, clap, it hit me: This guy can't go anywhere in town without being the king. It's a position in which very few ever find themselves.

"I have made myself approachable and I won't have it any other way," Griffin said. "I am a believer that you live your life the way you want to live it. You don't go hide out. You don't go doing all those things so people can't get to you. I want to live my life. I was born and raised here in Columbus, and when I walk down the streets I want to be able to walk down the streets. Yes, people ask for my autograph now and then but that's all right because I appreciate the fact that people remember me.

"It hasn't always been at the appropriate time but for the most part I try to accommodate."

If any Buckeye ever had reason to be a little enamored with himself, it's Griffin. He was a star at Eastmoor High School in Columbus, excelling at wrestling and track as well as on the gridiron. He set an Ohio State single-game rushing record in his first full game at the collegiate level. He went on to lead OSU in rushing four straight years as the Buckeyes won four Big Ten titles and made as many appearances in the Rose Bowl. He was a three-time All-American. And, by the way, he won the Heisman Trophy in 1974 and 1975, making him the first and only two-time winner of the prestigious award.

Through it all he has remained supremely humble. In fact he missed out on being named team MVP—and presumably Big Ten MVP for the third straight year—after his senior season by one vote. The difference? He cast his ballot for his roommate and best friend, quarterback Cornelius Greene.

Griffin played eight years for the Cincinnati Bengals and decided to accept an intermediary position as assistant director of staff employment at OSU in 1984. It was no glory detail—just put your head down and work. But eventually the athletic department decided to cash in by luring Griffin over as a "special assistant" to the athletic director. Oftentimes, that meant playing in golf outings with alumni and posing for pictures with gift-givers. And there were handshakes by the thousands, enough to awe a politician.

It wasn't the challenge Griffin was seeking, but he played along. He was named assistant athletic director in 1987 and eventually became associate AD in charge of thirteen men's and women's varsity sports. Most recently, he was named to head up the school's alumni association. But to this day Griffin remains OSU's unofficial ambassador of goodwill.

"You won't find them any nicer," said longtime local TV sports anchor and OSU announcer Jimmy Crum. "I don't

know of an enemy Archie has. He's got friends everywhere."

"That comes from his mom and dad, Margaret and James Griffin," Greene said from his Washington, D.C., home. "Archie doesn't know any other way to deal with people. He learned from the best. We played for Coach Hayes, who always stressed the importance of how to handle yourself on and off the field, and he was fortunate to come from a real quality home.

"His parents were churchgoing, they were strict, and they were respectful. They taught him to respect everyone. I learned a lot from him on that."

Duncan Griffin played with older brothers Archie and Ray at Ohio State in the 1970s. To this day he marvels at both Archie's undying celebrity and the way his brother has dealt with it.

"I have a lot of respect for Archie," he said. "The way he's developed himself as a person, the way he handles himself in public, and the way he's available to people is just incredible. I look at all my brothers and find things that stick out about each of them, and with Archie it's always been the way he handles himself. He's one of the most humble people I know."

Path to Greatness

Archie is one of eight children in his family. The first was James Jr., followed by Larry, Darryle, Archie, Ray, Duncan, Keith, and Krystal, seven boys who played football and a baby girl. Just two years younger than Archie, Ray was a more gifted natural athlete and often let Archie know about it.

"I didn't know I had speed, to be honest with you, until I got into eighth grade. I used to run against Ray and he'd always beat me," he said.

Archie was indeed fast. He anchored the relay teams for the Linmoor Junior High track team, which never lost a meet while Archie was in eighth and ninth grade. His group lost the 880-yard relay just one time when a team member dropped the baton.

"They [once] put us in the eighth lane because our qualifying time was the slowest and we won the city championship anyway," Archie recalled.

In ninth grade Griffin led his team to a championship in basketball. But it was football that allowed him to really distinguish himself.

He had played on the offensive line and at nose guard his first two years of organized ball—and sparingly at that. But in seventh grade when the team's fullback didn't show up for the first practice, Griffin volunteered to play the position. He made the league all-star team the next two years.

Learning to block and take a pounding at fullback, combined with the skills wrestling taught him, enabled Archie to hold up physically on the college football field. This training turned out to be invaluable for a guy who was labeled undersized his entire career. In fact Hayes attended several of Griffin's wrestling matches to be convinced that Griffin had the toughness to play football at OSU.

"I loved wrestling, and I always felt that wrestling helped me tremendously in my football," Archie said. "It gave me strength, balance, confidence, and mental toughness more than anything else, because it's a tough sport. Wrestling is the toughest sport I ever participated in, no question about it. It made me feel like I could take somebody on if I had to."

Griffin (rear) said he learned toughness on the wrestling mat in high school. (courtesy Archie Griffin)

Even at 5'7½" and 180 pounds as a high school senior, Archie could do just that. He starred at fullback at Eastmoor, although coach Bob Stuart occasionally called for the "Archie I," which shifted Griffin to tailback.

Griffin was being courted by lots of big schools but Hayes nipped that in the bud by making a big impression. Woody took the youngster to the Jai Lai restaurant, which is where he took all his recruits. The two of them talked for three hours.

When Archie got home he said, "Daddy, I don't think Coach Hayes wants me to play football for Ohio State."

"Why do you say that?" his father asked.

"Well, the whole time I was there we never talked about football. He wanted to talk about other things, mostly my academics," Archie said.

"Son," replied his father, "you go play football for that man."

Archie, of course, took the advice.

The start to Archie's unprecedented OSU career is now legendary. He was a fresh face in 1972, the first year the NCAA allowed freshmen to participate. Hayes had groused about the change in the off-season and all but promised to keep his newcomers glued to his bench. Still, he inserted Griffin into the season opener with Iowa.

Archie's number was called. While taking a pitchout he looked downfield to see how the blocking was set up—and promptly dropped the ball. "We recovered it but I came right out," Griffin said. "Knowing how much Coach Hayes hated fumbles and wasn't real fond of playing freshman, I thought, 'That's it. My season's over.' "

The team had two weeks to prepare for the second game of the season against North Carolina. Griffin used the time to try to make another impression as a reserve in practice. He had no idea he'd play. In fact he didn't even stay in the hotel with the team the night before the game.

Then, suddenly, Hayes called for the youngster.

"I couldn't find my helmet because I didn't think I'd get in," Griffin said. "I was in a daze the whole time. Thank goodness I knew my plays."

Griffin also knew how to hit the hole, make tacklers miss, and when to turn on the jets. His now-famous number 45 was a blur that late-September afternoon in the Horseshoe. He rolled up what was then a school record 239 yards rushing and helped OSU to an important 29–14 win.

"I remember we weren't running the ball particularly well early in the game," All-American lineman John Hicks said, "and their defensive end came up to me after a play and said,

Archie's Greatest Hits

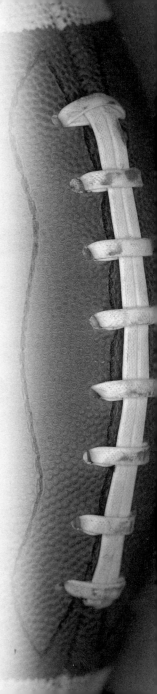

Archie Griffin's greatest accomplishments while at Ohio State (records and achievements as of the end of the 2002 season):

- Only two-time winner of the Heisman Memorial Trophy, winning the prized hardware in back-to-back years (1974 and 1975); also recognized as the national collegiate player of the year by winning the Walter Camp Award the same two years and the Maxwell Award in 1975
- Only player in OSU history to lead the team in yards rushing in four straight seasons
- OSU's all-time leading career rusher with 5,589 yards
- Set school single-game record with 239 yards rushing versus North Carolina as a freshman playing in his first full game
- Won the Big Ten Silver Football Award as MVP of the conference following the 1973 and 1974 seasons
- Led OSU to four Big Ten titles, including one outright in 1975
- Member of the National High School, Ohio State Athletics, Rose Bowl, Walter Camp, National Football Foundation, and College Football Halls of Fame
- Holds NCAA records with thirty-three total 100-yard games rushing, including thirty-one straight
- Holds NCAA record with a career average of 6.13 yards per carry
- Ranks fifth in NCAA rushing with 5,177 career yards

Note: The NCAA does not recognize statistics from bowl games.

'You guys up North can't block.' Later in the game, Archie was in there and running all over the place. I went up to the guy and told him, 'You guys from North Carolina can't tackle.'"

Hicks had gone to see the prodigy Griffin in high school and knew the Buckeyes had lassoed something special. Many others were soon convinced, too. "There was always a question in everybody's mind if he would make it or not," said Crum, now retired. "But after that game with North Carolina there was none. He was just a whirling dervish. You could just hear the oohs, ohs, and ahs in the press box."

Still, there were some skeptics who thought Griffin wouldn't have the durability to last in the brutal Big Ten. Griffin never worried about it.

"You know what, when you're that young you don't really think about size," said Griffin, who wore specially designed thigh pads to absorb the shock of all the hits he took. "Of course people told me I was too small to play at Ohio State. But what I always told people back was, 'Size doesn't matter. The game of football I play they don't open holes vertically. They open 'em horizontally. So what does size have to do with that?' The truth is I wasn't very big but I had to do battle with what the Lord gave me."

Even though Griffin realized playing running back was mostly instinctive, he still learned by watching other backs, especially on the finer points like blocking, protecting himself, stiff arming, and correct ball placement. Because Griffin grew up playing fullback he picked a pretty good role model on how to play: Jim Brown.

"He was the guy that I wanted to run like," he said.

Archie was deceptively strong and knew how to evade tacklers or make them tug harmlessly on his lower body. He also knew how to deliver a shot of his own to avoid absorbing lots of contact. And he had one other move in his repertoire.

"There's a time when you better fall," he said. "Think about it. If you're struggling to get away and there are five guys coming, knowing that you're not going to get out of there, you get what you can get and you get down."

Hayes knew right away Griffin was his meal ticket. Griffin averaged 5.5 yards per carry on his way to a team-best 867 yards as a freshman. His totals the next three years were 1,577 yards, 1,695 yards, and 1,450 yards.

"To do that you had to have a lot of good things in your favor, and one of them was all the great blocks I got," he said. "I played behind some great lines. I'll be the first to tell you. I mean we had several guys make All-America."

Griffin also had the privilege of playing with an all-time backfield. Greene was a trusted leader who was devastating running the option. He also developed into an accurate passer. Another classmate, Brian Baschnagel, was a perfect complement at wingback, able to run, catch, and make the key block on the outside. Big fullback Pete Johnson was a punishing lead blocker and touchdown machine who usually got to put the exclamation point on drives. At the end of the 2002 season, Johnson still held school marks for season and career scoring. He scored a Big Ten record twenty-six touchdowns in 1975, the year of Archie's second Heisman.

"We had games where four backs, I mean all of them—the quarterback, halfback, fullback, and wingback—would get a hundred yards," Griffin said. "It was that good. It was that special."

But Griffin was the motor. OSU posted a 40–5–1 record in his four years, mostly because no one could stop him. With Griffin as the focal point, the line was challenged to make room for him every time out. Hayes would settle for nothing else.

"With Archie back there, first and foremost you wanted to hit your block because you had to answer to the old man if Arch got hurt," Hicks said. "He just elevated the whole team when he was doing his thing. I wish I could say I got to stand there and marvel at him but you were too busy knocking your guy down. It looked good on film, though."

How consistent was Griffin's brilliance? He rushed for 100 or more yards thirty-three times, including thirty-one straight. Both accomplishments are still NCAA records.

"The thing about that is Woody took him out of there as soon as things were in hand," Hicks said. "Archie probably played four full games his whole career—and he still set the NCAA record."

Bond That Remains Just As Strong

Griffin's jersey was retired on October 30, 1999, at halftime of an Ohio State–Iowa football game. How appropriate that was: It was on the very field he once roamed at OSU, playing the first opponent he'd faced as a Buckeye. And Griffin was there because he thought the ceremony was simply to honor one of his teams, the 1974 Buckeyes of twenty-five years earlier.

Griffin always felt most proud of his team accomplishments. "I think one of the big things people appreciate during the years that we played was we never lost in Ohio Stadium, so those fans that came to see us never saw us lose," he said. "Plus, in that time we didn't lose to Michigan. I think a lot of people in that group, not just me, are well respected because of that."

But when number 45 was hung up forever and Griffin's name affixed to the concrete of Ohio Stadium, the fans had a new way to continue their love affair with Archie. Holding a framed jersey handed to him by Athletic Director Andy Geiger

Griffin waited twenty years to welcome another Buckeye into the Heisman Trophy fraternity. He was on hand to congratulate 1995 winner Eddie George. (Brockway Sports Photos)

and standing next to the youngest of his three sons, Adam, Archie choked on tears as the crowd roared for a full two minutes.

There was just one thing missing from that moment: Cornelius Greene. Unable to come to the team reunion because he attended a funeral, Greene only heard about the magic of that day.

"It sounded like it was a great scene," said Greene, who has been a youth counselor most of his adult life. "I thought it was long overdue. I know Ohio State had a policy for a long time of not doing that but how could you give anyone that jersey number. I mean, we're talking about Archie Griffin."

Greene and Griffin would have been roommates if such procedures were done in alphabetical order. But they were paired together for a more obvious reason—they were just two of the three African Americans new to the program when they arrived. The other was backup running back Woodrow Roach.

Griffin was a conservative kid from a big family who did things by the book. Greene wore a big Afro and snazzy clothes and drove around a car with the license plate "Flam 7." They couldn't have been tighter.

"We were inseparable," Greene said. "Archie got a lot of my personality and I got some of his as well. I think we hit it off on day one. Archie had the record player and I had a TV. It was the best of both worlds."

On Sundays Archie took Cornelius to the modest east side home where he grew up, and where his parents still live. "His mom was like a surrogate mom to me. And his dad was very supportive of me, too," Greene said. "We used to take our laundry over there and have a home-cooked meal. Man, was that always a good day."

Greene was a flashy athlete throughout his career but he learned through the Griffins to calm his emotions. Even with opposing teams trying to take shots at him, Archie always was levelheaded. "Dad used to say you can't be focused enough if you're mad," Archie's brother Duncan said. "He'd say, 'If you let someone get in your head you're beat.'"

Of course there wasn't a whole lot of reason to be mad out on the field. With Greene at the controls and Griffin taking pitchouts, defenses were at the mercy of the Ohio State attack.

"He was something running that option, boy," Griffin said with a smile. "He could tuck that ball into your stomach, yank it right back out, spin, and just take off. It was really impressive."

Their destiny seemed set when the two, as seniors,

> "He's a better young man than he is a football player, and he's the best football player I've ever seen."
> —Woody Hayes on Archie Griffin

made the Rose Bowl for the fourth straight year and Ohio State, the nation's number one team, was favored to take out upstart UCLA and head coach Dick Vermeil. It didn't happen. The Bruins upset OSU 23–10, crushing national championship dreams. Griffin and Greene walked off the field overcome with emptiness.

"It's disbelief," Greene said. "We had beaten UCLA soundly earlier in the year. We just didn't play a great game. To this day Archie and I are haunted by that."

When Ohio State won the national championship at the 2003 Fiesta Bowl, Greene called Griffin's cell phone to congratulate the associate AD on finally getting the ring the two of them just missed decades earlier.

"He called me back the next morning as the team was getting on the bus and you could just hear the joy in his voice. It was unbelievable," Greene said. "I know if I were there in person we would have been hugging each other right at that moment."

Greene visits his buddy when he can and stays with Archie, wife Bonita, and sons Anthony, Andre, and Adam. Cornelius is Andre's godfather and Archie is the same for Cornelius's son Jason.

"Archie knows that if I were to die tomorrow I would want him to be involved in my kids' lives," Greene said.

"There's nobody else in the world I love more than Archie."

Defensive Back U.?

istorically, Ohio State has been blessed with as much talent as any program in the country. All-Americans seem to fall off of trees in Columbus, which is maybe why they are honored in arboreal fashion in the Buckeye Grove outside Ohio Stadium. Perhaps not fully appreciated in this mile-deep talent pool is the flood of great defensive backs who have worn scarlet and gray.

It's a tradition that did not begin with but certainly was enhanced by the arrival of Jack Tatum, who proved that even guys in the last line of defense can have a large hand in shutting down an offense.

"That's a trademark for Ohio State," Tatum said from his California home. "To play defensive back for the Buckeyes you've got to be a decent cover guy, but you also have to be a guy who's not afraid to come up and make the hit and make the tackle.

"The tackling in the NFL right now, it's terrible. There aren't that many DBs that make good form tackles and keep the play from being a big play. That's why you see so many Buckeyes in that league, because they're not afraid to do it."

Tatum was the least afraid of all. He played in perhaps the greatest era of OSU football (1968–70) and was probably the most menacing DB in Ohio State history. But certainly, there have been several standouts in more recent years, guys I had the pleasure of watching develop into All-American caliber players.

From 1950 until the spring of 2001 — basically half a century — the Buckeyes had fifty-three players taken in the first round of the NFL draft, almost one per year. A dozen of them played defensive back at Ohio State, an astounding figure, especially when you consider the first round generally is much heavier on linemen and offensive skill players.

Especially noteworthy is the five-year span beginning with Shawn Springs in 1997 (Seattle), then Antoine Winfield in 1999 (Buffalo), Ahmed Plummer in 2000 (San Francisco), and Nate Clements in 2001 (Buffalo). These picks vaulted OSU's reputation at defensive back into orbit.

Little Big Man

I can still remember trekking over to the Woody Hayes Athletic Center for the first day of freshman practice in 1995. John Cooper had ushered in another bumper crop of prospects and I wanted to get a peek at these prodigies myself.

There was this one newcomer I was hoping to get a close look at, a pipsqueak named Antoine Winfield who was jazzing up what threatened to be a mundane afternoon.

I had a hunch this Winfield kid was going to be someone to follow closely after hearing about his great career at Akron Garfield and talking to him on the phone during the recruiting period. When I saw he had been assigned number 11, my favorite number, I had even more expectations that he would be a player.

After about forty-five minutes, I was blown away. Winfield, despite being even smaller than his listed size of 5'10" and 187 pounds, was whapping guys to the indoor carpet on contact drills. He broke up passes. He showed catch-up speed down the field. He did each drill with a certain pep and a high level of effectiveness. He did it all with that smile on his face.

Dynamite comes in small packages: Antoine Winfield.
(Steve Helwagen/Buckeye Sports Bulletin)

I've been to a lot of practices and I've been more interested in watching the grass grow at some of them, but this one was different. It's often hard to tell if a freshman is going to pan out, and if he does, it's even harder to predict the timetable. In this case it was obvious. Winfield had the glow.

The only problem from Winfield's point of view—and not Cooper's—was that the Buckeyes were loaded at defensive back when he set foot on campus. It didn't take long for him to realize he was going to have to be exceptional even to earn time. He had to settle for a nickelback role at first until he could prove his cover skills. From there it was a journey to stardom beyond what anyone could have predicted.

While the Buckeyes were beating the likes of Washington, Notre Dame, and Penn State in 1995 en route to earning a number one ranking, the offense was gaining plenty of notoriety with Eddie George and Bobby Hoying being touted as Heisman candidates, Terry Glenn playing as well as any receiver in the country, Rickey Dudley coming into stardom at tight end, and Orlando Pace securing his reputation as a topflight tackle. But the defense wasn't a can of hash, either. The front seven had lots of experience and hustle with warriors like Mike Vrabel, Matt Finkes, Luke Fickell, and Greg Bellisari. At defensive back, a perceived weakness going in to the year, the Buckeyes proved to be rife with impressive talent, albeit young.

Early on, Shawn Springs was getting more publicity than anyone in the secondary, but after seeing the young Winfield perform in practice he told reporters, "Hey, I'm trying to hold onto my job." Springs, of course, didn't lose his post at corner. He went on to be a qualified star in 1995 and 1996. But his point was well taken. With youngsters like Winfield, Plummer, Ty Howard, and Damon Moore in the secondary, a new era of DB greatness was about to unfold.

The best of that bunch—and arguably the greatest defensive back of all time at Ohio State—was Winfield, OSU's Little Big Man. He became Ohio State's first winner of the Thorpe Award, which honors the best DB in the nation, in December 1998, the twilight of his phenomenal collegiate career.

Winfield apparently shrunk in those years since I first saw him—he was listed 5'9", 180 as a senior. OSU fans never would have seen that great Thorpe Award season if it weren't for his slight frame. A "larger" Winfield would have been a very highly regarded commodity by the NFL. But there was something about proving people wrong that appealed to Winfield, who otherwise came across as the most agreeable young man you'd ever meet.

"People told me I was too small in high school to play high school ball and I heard that when I was ready to go to college, too," Winfield once told me during an interview in which we literally saw each other eye to eye. "I'm sure I'll hear it in the pros and I'll keep hearing it."

Playing for a team that just missed winning the national title and gaining so much notoriety in 1998, Winfield still couldn't match his mind-boggling output of 1997, during which he logged a team-high one hundred tackles, an almost sick figure for a cornerback.

Early in his tenure at OSU, Cooper used to rave about the prowess of safety David Fulcher, whom he coached at Arizona State (and who went on to stardom in the NFL with the Cincinnati Bengals). But it didn't take long into Antoine's career for Cooper to brand him as the best DB he'd ever coached.

In the regular-season finale of 1997, I saw Michigan's Charles Woodson record three big plays in UM's win over Ohio State: an interception in the end zone, a long gainer on offense running a dig route, and a punt return for a touchdown. After such a crowning moment against the rival Buckeyes, voters could see his all-around play had an enormous impact on Michigan's undefeated season and decided it was time to elect a defensive player as winner of the Heisman Trophy.

There's only one problem. Woodson wasn't the best corner on the field that day. It was the little guy in white with 11 on his back who kept disrupting plays and blasting ball carriers. With Winfield breaking up passes and stuffing the run like an All-American linebacker, Michigan gained exactly 42 rushing yards on forty-two carries.

Although Winfield didn't receive the national acclaim Woodson did in 1997, he was elected team MVP by his teammates after the season. The following year, he claimed Woodson's Thorpe Award. After Winfield won the award, Cooper, the coach who stumped for him to be so honored for two years, said, "We've had some great defensive backs here, guys like Shawn Springs, Ty Howard, and Marlon Kerner. There were some great defensive backs who played here before I came. There are a bunch of them on the wall in there as All-Americans.

"But we've never had a Thorpe Award winner. I don't know if we've ever had one as good as Antoine Winfield."

Added Moore: "He just totally shuts down the other team's top receiver. When you look over at his side, you know he's going to take care of his guy and make it just ten on ten out there."

But to do that and be such a force against the run while stifling receivers after the catch is what's really unheard of for a corner—and why you could say that he had just as great an impact as the man still perceived as OSU's greatest-ever DB,

Tatum. In fact Winfield left OSU as the only nonlinebacker and just fifth Buckeye ever to record at least 200 solo tackles. Incidentally, tackles were not part of official statistics until 1970, meaning Tatum's career sophomore and junior numbers are not known. But, for comparison sake, Tatum was credited with forty-nine tackles as a senior.

Born for Stardom

The only reason why Winfield's career was not considered even more astounding is that it overlapped that of Springs, who, like Tatum, proved in three years on the gridiron that he was an all-time great. However, Springs was not the same type of player as Winfield. In fact, other than the magnetic personality, they were very different. While Winfield was an Ohio boy who had to make much of his reputation, Springs was a high school phenom with size, 4.3 speed, and an ideal pedigree — his father, Ron, played for the Buckeyes under Woody Hayes. Shawn was an impressionable youngster when his father played for the Dallas Cowboys. Among the players who became surrogate uncles for him were Everson Walls and Tony Dorsett.

Shawn grew up around football and knew the NFL locker room well. He just seemed destined for the same life. Even his high school, which sounded like it already was named after him, Silver Spring (Maryland) Springbrook, seemed to suggest Springs was can't miss. He was.

It's hard to believe now, though, that Springs nearly played for the Maize and Blue. In fact he had given a verbal commitment to Michigan coach Gary Moeller and also was smitten with Penn State for a while, noting a batch of delicious cookies Suzanne Paterno had baked him. But Springs eventually

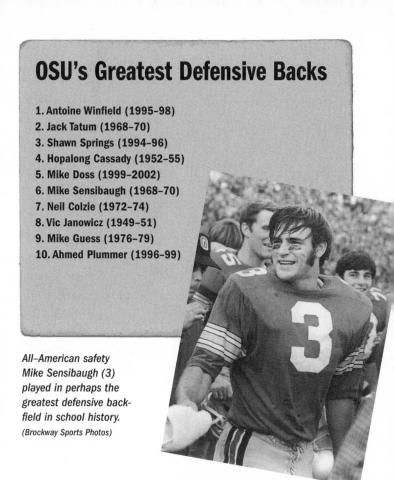

OSU's Greatest Defensive Backs

1. Antoine Winfield (1995–98)
2. Jack Tatum (1968–70)
3. Shawn Springs (1994–96)
4. Hopalong Cassady (1952–55)
5. Mike Doss (1999–2002)
6. Mike Sensibaugh (1968–70)
7. Neil Colzie (1972–74)
8. Vic Janowicz (1949–51)
9. Mike Guess (1976–79)
10. Ahmed Plummer (1996–99)

All–American safety Mike Sensibaugh (3) played in perhaps the greatest defensive back-field in school history.
(Brockway Sports Photos)

signed with OSU in 1993. By the end of 1996, he had been named to several All-America teams and was selected as the defensive player of the year in the Big Ten. That type of honor was unheard of for a corner to that point, but it was obvious Springs's sticky cover abilities played a major hand in OSU's aggressive press-up defense that was just becoming all the rage.

Blessed with ideal cover corners like Springs, Winfield, and Howard, first-year coordinator Fred Pagac went for the throat with as many as nine players on the attack, and the ploy worked to near perfection. Springs became one of the most valuable players in the league without doing much in the box score. Receivers couldn't get free of him and opposing offenses couldn't handle OSU's blitz schemes.

Football had to reach well into the 1990s before followers of the sport could fully realize the true worth of a great, shut-down corner. Unfortunately, it probably took the hype machine surrounding the chest-thumping Deion Sanders for it to happen. But, of course, guys like Springs, who once claimed Everson Walls as his hero, loved the newfound attention.

I can honestly say I've never covered an athlete as affable or as ticketed for the professional ranks as Shawn Springs, who had a rare combination of talent, flamboyance, and humility. You just got the sense the whole time he was at Ohio State that he was fully aware he was there merely to enjoy himself and pass time until the NFL came calling. Not even a redshirt in 1993 could slow him down. Springs learned determination and technique under defensive backs coach Larry Coker in 1993 and 1994. He then flourished under the direction and positive reinforcement of new secondary coach Lovie Smith in 1995. When the gruff and demanding Jon Tenuta took over the position in 1996, Springs was equipped to take it, and his game rose into the stratosphere.

When it became evident Springs was set to declare for the 1997 NFL draft, I called his father, who told me, "This was a situation where Shawn could not get any better at Ohio State. The toughest thing I had to do was go out and motivate him to go out and play every week because offenses wouldn't even throw the ball to his side. It's frustrating."

Ron was speaking nothing but absolute truth. Cornerback is about as easy a thing to do as tying your shoes while you're running the 40-yard dash. But Shawn had it down so cold he sometimes looked like he was gliding on the gridiron.

Of course there were those who sharply criticized Springs, saying he was letting down himself and the program by leaving early. But even many of those people had to know deep down that their comments were merely selfish. Springs was ripe, and being the third overall pick confirmed it in a hurry. And unlike others to jump ship, he did so with a deep appreciation of his alma mater.

At the press conference to announce the early exit of himself and Orlando Pace, Shawn's broad smile was on display. So was his goofball demeanor as he yukked it up for reporters and interrupted himself to ask Pace, "How do you like my speech so far, O?" But Springs's voice shook when he recognized teammates in attendance such as fellow defensive backs Ty Howard and Anthony Gwinn and quarterback Stanley Jackson.

"They're like my brothers," Springs said.

Unfortunately, some will remember Springs for one of the most disastrous plays in OSU history. With the undefeated Buckeyes trying to protect a 9–0 lead at home against hated Michigan, Springs slipped on the Ohio Stadium field and couldn't recover on a long Tai Streets touchdown. The third-quarter play shifted momentum and set the stage for a 13–9 UM upset of number two Ohio State. But only a very select few got to see the humbled Springs as I did after the game. He came up to the interview room in the southeast tower of the stadium, answered every question as stand-up as you can be, and even chatted with me a little after that.

He admitted being a little cocky before the game and telling teammates how he was going to silence Streets. Even after a bitter defeat that cost him a shot at the national championship in his final season, Springs realized he learned a valuable lesson.

"Don't talk trash. That's it," he told me.

When I saw Springs last he'd attended the 2002 spring intrasquad game and handed a $100,000 check to Andy Geiger, OSU's AD, to head up the Shawn Springs/Majority of One Postgraduate Scholarship.

"It's like investing into something that's been invested into you," he told me right after the presentation. "It's more than just giving money to the university. I'm blessed to be in the situation I am, and it's because of Ohio State and the people that are here. It's like giving back to your family."

Springs, by the way, later took a correspondence course at the University of Washington to finish up his bachelor's degree. This from a guy who always knew he was going to make it in the NFL.

Plum of a Player

How high a standard did Springs and Winfield set for the corner position? So high that when Winfield was a senior people often referred to Ahmed Plummer as the "other" corner, like he was some sort of weak link.

"He is probably one of the most overlooked corners in the country," Tenuta said going into the 1998 season.

Plummer's flawless technique and coachable approach made him a reluctant star in the late 1990s. OSU was a woeful 6–6 in 1999, not the kind of send-off Plummer was looking for as a cocaptain. But the gentlemanly product of Cincinnati was all smiles at the team's postseason banquet. He was honored for being named All-American and was singled out by the team for academic excellence. He also won the Arnie Chonko Award as the team's top defensive back and the Bill Willis Award as the top defender. But what really showed Plummer's worth was winning two prestigious awards that were voted on by the players: the team MVP award and the Bo Rein Award signifying the team's most inspirational player.

"Those kinds of awards mean the most to you because we've been through so much together and we're so close. That's a lot of love," Plummer told me.

Plummer winning was no surprise, though, considering his popularity with all those around him. Simply put, he was the epitome of class. In fact he made himself available to me after he was drafted by granting an impromptu interview at his church. Plummer had gone there to pray and celebrate after being chosen in the first round by the 49ers.

By 1998, when the Buckeyes threatened to post a wire-to-wire national championship, people were beginning to figure out special things were happening in OSU's defensive backfield. That year, in fact, *Sports Illustrated* ran a feature on the topic, entitled "First-Rate Secondary."

"Stacked with speedsters who hit hard and smother receivers, Ohio State's defensive backfield is the strongest unit on the nation's best team," read the subhead. The story was accompanied by a photo of Winfield, Plummer, Moore, safety Gary Berry, and nickelback Central McClellion. All five went on to play in the NFL.

While Penn State had dubbed itself "Linebacker U.," Ohio State had a similar reputation with so many star middle linebackers who excelled in OSU's traditional 4–3 scheme in the 1970s and 1980s. But in that same stretch of time, the Buckeyes probably had as many standout defensive backs. Mike Sensibaugh, Tim Anderson, Neil Colzie, Tim Fox, and

Chris Gamble (7) and Mike Doss (2) have earned national recognition in recent years, but are in a long line of accomplished Ohio State defensive backs. (Jeff Brehm)

Ray Griffin all made All-American in the 1970s; the 1980s featured standouts such as Garcia Lane, Sonny Gordon, and William White. By the time Cooper had the reins in 1988, it was a given that OSU would feature a playmaker in the secondary every year. In the 1990s defensive backs were doing untold things in Columbus. Moore became the first nonlinebacker to lead the team in tackles when he recorded eighty-nine in 1996. Winfield had his even one hundred the next season, and Moore returned to the throne in 1998 with eighty-one total tackles. Outside linebacker Na'il Diggs broke the trend with a team-best ninety-four stops in 1999, but a smallish safety by the name of Mike Doss took the reins of the defense in 2000 (ninety-four) and 2001 (eighty-seven), the latter under new head coach Jim Tressel.

When the importance of fine play from the last line of defense became even more crucial as the game evolved, people knew where to go: Florida and Texas, where speed ruled, and Ohio, the birthplace of football and state with the most respect for the game. Out west where football is more wide open and in the East where talent is more scarce, it's very common for the best athletes and players to be used at the offensive skill positions first. In the Midwest there is no shame whatsoever in playing, say, strong safety. In fact you've got to prove yourself worthy and tough to take on that assignment.

It's no coincidence that Ohio has churned out secondary talent from the high school ranks for decades now. In recent years the trend has only solidified (Michigan's Woodson, by the way, is from Freemont, Ohio). Certainly, the Buckeye State has been good to Ohio State when it comes to defensive backs. The Akron–Canton area alone has produced Winfield, Fox, Doss, and many others. Sensibaugh and Plummer are among those from Cincinnati. Columbus has turned out more secondary men than anyone can count, the most notable being Heisman Trophy winner Howard "Hopalong" Cassady, who was an outstanding defensive back as well as offensive weapon, along with Griffin, Howard, Mike Guess, and Roger Harper. Still others from various outposts of Ohio were Fred Bruney, Ted Provost, Nate Clements, and William White.

Rover, Monster, Assassin

But the fiercest and perhaps the best Buckeye ever to roam the secondary was Jack Tatum, an imposing figure from Passaic, New Jersey, number 32. Tatum was a 6', 202-pound wrecking ball when he made his OSU debut in 1968. He was one of the "Super Sophs," part of a recruiting class that still is considered the best ever at Ohio State—the very group that piloted the Buckeyes to the 1968 national championship.

Originally recruited as a linebacker and running back, Tatum also dabbled as a punt returner. He once returned a punt roughly 60 yards for a touchdown in a team scrimmage, yet still drew the ire of coach Woody Hayes after dashing, darting, and twisting through the cover team.

"You run north and south, dammit!" Hayes yelled at the frosh. "You play defense from now on."

Tatum quickly assumed the role of roverback, sometimes referred to as "monsterback" in Hayes's system, and redefined the position by playing it with a recklessness not seen before or since. Surprisingly, Tatum had not yet been inducted into the College Football Hall of Fame as of the end of 2002 although he was a listed candidate in 2000.

The credentials certainly are there. Tatum was a two-time All-American and was named the national Defensive Player of the Year after the 1970 season. In the NFL, Tatum played nine years and was a mainstay for the Oakland Raiders. He's one of the very few players to go on to that level from Ohio State and gain a nasty reputation (his book, *They Call Me Assassin*, was a bestseller). Unfortunately, Tatum is best known by many as the safety who paralyzed New England Patriots receiver Darryl Stingley in a preseason game. But he was a three-year Pro Bowl selection who helped the Raiders win a Super Bowl in 1976.

At Ohio State, Tatum shut down every player with a big

Some believe the menacing-looking Jack Tatum was the best DB in college football. (Brockway Sports Photos)

reputation who dared enter his path. O. J. Simpson, Leroy Keyes, Ed Podolak—he slammed them all. And that was just in his sophomore season. By the time he was through he was the most feared defender in the nation.

Villain or not, Tatum would have to be considered the best safety ever to play at Ohio State and, many say, the best defensive back.

"I never had really tried to sort that out," Tatum said, "but I know opposing teams would change their offense because of me so that has to mean something. I always lined up protecting the wide side of the field and teams would run away from me and run to the short side. But I didn't mind that because the other guys could all make plays, and they did."

Tatum would have had an impact on any defensive backfield in the country by himself, but not coincidentally he reached the apex at his position because he played with other great defensive backs. In fact his classmates—defensive halfback Tim Anderson and safety Mike Sensibaugh—and halfback Ted Provost, who was a year ahead, all earned All-American honors at some point in their careers. Provost, who is best remembered at OSU for a game-turning play in the 1968 upset of Purdue, was a seventh-round draft pick of the Los Angeles Rams in 1970. The following year, Anderson joined Tatum in the first round of the draft when he was tabbed by the San Francisco 49ers. Sensibaugh went in the eighth round to the Kansas City Chiefs that same year.

Even with all this talent, the young secondary coach often took the brunt of Woody's wrath in 1968. But the constructive criticism didn't seem to hurt because that coach was Lou Holtz. Many great budding coaches have taken over the position in the following years, another reason why the production of the secondary has been so consistent. But Tatum was one of those supreme athletes who needed no extra motivation from a coach. In other words, he was extremely rare.

I remember a fairly chaotic scene as a reporter in 1998. The 1968 team was celebrating its thirty-year reunion as part of halftime festivities of one of the home games. My editor asked me to claw my way down to the field to grab an old player or two for an interview. Once I spotted Tatum I knew I had the ideal person. While I was asking Tatum a few harmless questions, the team began to push in on the sideline anticipating taking the field for the halftime ceremonies. It was getting pretty tight. I put my right hand on Tatum's shoulder to gain my balance and he grabbed me by the forearm as I almost fell. I couldn't believe it—at fifty, the guy felt like a piece of iron. His freakish accomplishments on the field started to make sense.

A moment later, Tatum noticed his old buddy Anderson and lunged to get his attention—and caught me flush in the face, by accident.

I immediately felt two things—woozy and privileged.

How else would you feel if you just got smacked in the chops by Jack Tatum?

A Rose Has Its Thorn, Then Blooms

"Success isn't permanent, and failure isn't fatal."
—*Mike Ditka*

"If you want a place in the sun, prepare to put up with a few blisters."
—*Abigail Van Buren*

Indiana State Route 37 never looked so alive.

Usually, it's a drab stretch of road that leads travelers from the south end of the Indianapolis outerbelt down to Hoosier country, better known as Bloomington. But on this day— November 16, 1996—the causeway had a different look. A majority of the southbound vehicles had Ohio license plates and most all of them had some sort of Ohio State decor, be it pennants in the windows of RVs, buckeye nut necklaces and Brutus Buckeye dolls on dashboards, or Ohio State logos on car flags flapping in the cool, overcast air.

OSU fans, as they are wont to do for big games within driving distance of Columbus, were out in force. But the real sign that this was anything but just another road game was the opportunists who were selling roses along the side of the road.

The undefeated Buckeyes were on the verge of clinching a long-overdue berth in the Rose Bowl and all they had to do to snare it was take down an Indiana team that had lost fourteen straight Big Ten games. However, like all things of great significance, it didn't come easy.

The Hoosiers were still a gritty bunch and would be giving their all for their fallen leader, Bill Mallory, in his last home game as IU head coach. Mallory's firing was announced on Halloween and the team promised to rally around him. Ironically, Mallory also was very well liked and respected in Columbus, mostly because he was an assistant to Woody Hayes and helped the Buckeyes to the 1968 national championship.

As the game unfolded, it looked for a while like the Buckeye fans would need all those roses to dab their eyes. With Indiana playing way over its head, the game was tied at ten midway through the fourth quarter.

"People like to say they're not nervous in sports. Well, I was nervous the whole game," outspoken wide receiver Dimitrious Stanley said. "But I also knew we had a lot of guys who could make that one play that changes the game."

In 1996 most of those guys resided on the defensive side of the ball. Sure enough, freshman middle linebacker Andy Katzenmoyer stripped the ball from IU quarterback Jay Rodgers with 6:18 to play, and defensive end Matt Finkes grabbed it out of the air and took off. Finkes was running to the south end zone but looked like he could have made a right-hand turn and headed all the way to Pasadena.

Strong safety Damon Moore took over from there as Indiana tried to play catch-up. His fumble recovery on the ensuing possession set up a game-clinching field goal by Josh Jackson, and he returned an interception for a touchdown that served as the exclamation point on a 27–17 win.

Buckeye fans were so elated their team was going to the Rose Bowl for the first time in twelve seasons that they trampled

Ohio State fans take over Memorial Stadium in Bloomington, Indiana, after their beloved Buckeyes clinch the school's first Rose Bowl berth in a dozen years. (Steve Helwagen/Buckeye Sports Bulletin)

down a chain-link fence near the end zone, ripped down the goalposts, partied on the field, and hoisted several of their heroes in the air in the Bloomington dusk.

When told Indiana University officials were honked off about the damage, Athletic Director Andy Geiger unapologetically replied, "We'll pay for it."

Coach John Cooper, who had taken serious heat for missing out on the Rose Bowl the previous three seasons with what was deemed superior talent, answered postgame questions with lipstick marks on his cheek from his wife, Helen.

Finally, it appeared, Cooper had put together a team that couldn't be stopped.

The Buildup

Ironically, OSU wasn't supposed to be flirting with a championship in 1996. The team lost some of its more decorated players of all-time after the 1995 campaign, including Heisman Trophy–winning running back Eddie George, record-breaking quarterback Bobby Hoying, athletically gifted tight end Rickey Dudley, and wideout Terry Glenn, who left early for the NFL after winning the Biletnikoff Award. Glenn, Dudley, and George were all NFL first-rounders with Glenn and Dudley going in the first nine picks.

Even though the Buckeyes were ranked in the top ten of the Associated Press poll to start the season one had to wonder if that was more on reputation. Even with the ranking, the 1996 Buckeyes felt slapped by all the guarded predictions.

"Our class was very tight, and we were determined to go out on a good note," said Stanley, a senior from nearby Worthington. "People thought we lost everything without Bobby, Eddie, and Terry. They wondered how our offense was going to be any good. I didn't see it that way at all. I knew we had a lot of talent."

Stanley's strong hunch was correct. In fact the "decimated" Buckeyes went out and cooked Rice 70–7 in the season opener. In the romp they showed there were indeed capable replacements on offense, specifically freshmen Michael Wiley and David Boston.

Wiley scored a touchdown all three times he touched the ball—a 49-yard reverse and receptions of 51 and 60 yards. A hulking 6'3", Boston won the receiver spot opposite Stanley and scored four touchdowns in the first two games, including a 66-yard punt return with just eight Buckeyes on the field in a 72–0 destruction of Pitt.

A smaller and quicker back than George, Pepe Pearson quickly showed he could get the job done at tailback. OSU also was getting favorable results with a platoon system at quarterback. Junior starter Stanley Jackson was an exceptional athlete with a big arm and scrambling ability, but quiet sophomore Joe Germaine had the accuracy and command to take over when more of a passing game was needed.

Boston and the emergence of Stanley seemed to make up for the loss of Glenn, who had amassed gaudy marks of 1,411 receiving yards, an average of 22.1 yards per catch, and a school-record seventeen TDs in 1995.

The offensive line was in strong hands, too, especially with Orlando Pace, a nimble human eclipse at 6'6" and 320 pounds, manning the all-important left tackle spot. Pace's job was simple: anchor the line, open up even bigger holes for Pearson, and provide blind-side protection for Jackson and Germaine despite their completely opposite styles.

Still, what made OSU a national championship contender that season was its stellar defense. Cooper's first step to that end was to upgrade Fred Pagac, a no-bull coach who played in the height of the Woody Hayes era, to defensive coordinator.

Pagac put Katzenmoyer, the USA Today prep defensive player of the year while at nearby Westerville South High School, into the middle of his 4–3 defense that he termed "The Silver Bullets." Wearing the number 45 that Archie Griffin made famous and flanked by heady 'backers Greg Bellisari and Ryan Miller, Katzenmoyer didn't disappoint. In fact he was a perfect fit for Pagac's constant attack mode.

The defensive line was blessed with savvy veterans who had a knack for getting in the backfield, especially ends Finkes and Mike Vrabel. Meanwhile, the secondary was deep and talented.

Shawn Springs was a qualified star at one corner and Ty Howard was emerging as a lockdown guy in his own right. With those two able to guard receivers by themselves, Pagac often called for Moore to cheat up at strong safety and Rob Kelly to play a kamikaze free safety. Another defensive back proved worthy of key playing time—young Antoine Winfield.

It was this band of Bullets that stunned fifth-ranked Notre Dame in South Bend, 29–16, and never let up in a 38–7 romp over number four Penn State in Ohio Stadium.

This, of course, was jaw dropping. The Associated Press pollsters moved the Buckeyes to number two, where they would stay the rest of the season.

However, the games got a little tougher. OSU had to escape its own environs with a 17–14 win over Wisconsin and fell behind 14–0 at Purdue the next week before waking up.

"I think we were too confident at the beginning of games," Stanley said. "But after 70–7 and 72–0 and the way we won some of those early games, how could you not be? We'd get into this pattern where we'd come out too confident early, run the ball like s__t and then throw it like we had to."

The Slip-Up

That pattern continued in the scare with the Hoosiers. But with that huge win out of the way, OSU fans thought the pressure would be relieved.

By clinching the Rose Bowl berth before taking on rival Michigan in the regular-season finale, the Buckeyes accomplished something done by just one OSU team prior: the 1957 Buckeyes. That squad still took out Michigan, won the Rose Bowl, and captured a national championship.

Better yet, OSU was hosting the Wolverines, who looked to have their most mediocre team in years. Undefeated seasons went up in smoke in the 1993 and 1995 Big Ten finales but those games were staged in Ann Arbor. Early betting lines had the Buckeyes as seventeen-point favorites. Many believed OSU was going to break the Michigan hex in resounding fashion.

All signs pointed to the dream season continuing. Then, those guys with the funny stripes on their maize-and-blue helmets came to town.

The evening before The Game, Ohio State held a very public Senior Tackle. Instead of a sendoff for the players in their last year of eligibility, though, the event turned into a pep rally fueled by guest speaker Earle Bruce. Dressed in his trademark black jacket and fedora, the former OSU coach sauntered around pointing and yelling at players and riling up the approximately 20,000 fans in Ohio Stadium who braved the cold.

"You've been great, but to be great at Ohio State you've got to beat Michigan," he barked into a microphone.

As usual for a big game, OSU decided to pour on tradition like sugar in a frosting factory. Players ran through the Tunnel of Pride. The OSU marching band put on its top pregame show of the year. Fans cut their tailgating short to pack the stadium well before kickoff.

The first bad sign came as team captain Bellisari, the last senior, was announced to the crowd. He was nearly trampled by the Wolverines, who decided to race to their east sideline as Bellisari was making his way to his parents, rose in hand.

Then, it was announced that Cooper was flip-flopping the lineup and would start Germaine at QB over Jackson. Germaine had played almost all of the Indiana contest. Jackson was in a three-game slump.

"I didn't agree with it from the start," Dimitrious Stanley said. "I always respected Coach Cooper, he did a lot of good things here, but that was a move I just didn't understand. To

Joe Cool Saves the Day

He was as apple pie as they come. Joe Germaine actually said things like "geez" and "shucks." He kept his hair boy-scout short. He never raised his voice. In fact it usually was barely audible.

There were times at Ohio State when Germaine, a polite Arizona boy, looked like he might not get a real chance to grab hold of the starting quarterback job despite his precision and knowledge of the playbook. Some around the program thought Germaine was too nice to complain when he shared time as a sophomore and junior with Stanley Jackson.

But Germaine simply made the most of his opportunities. When the 1997 Rose Bowl was up for grabs, it was Germaine who got to duel at the end with Arizona State's Jake "The Snake" Plummer. It was Germaine who played the hero with a last-minute scoring drive that earned him most outstanding player honors and forever endeared him to Buckeye fans.

"I imagine I'll always be associated with that, which is fine," he said. "It was a great honor just to play in that game and to win it was a thrill. It doesn't bother me at all if that's the way people remember me."

Ironically, Germaine, once a draft pick of the Colorado Rockies, is a Mesa, Arizona, native who grew up a Sun Devils fan. However, his hometown school only gave him a cursory look and recruited him as a defensive back. Still holding out hope of being a quarterback at a big-time school, Germaine headed off to Scottsdale Community College. After a record-setting freshman season there during which he once completed forty-nine passes in a game, he got an offer from Ohio State, made by head coach John Cooper.

"When I was in junior college, the last place I thought I'd come to was Ohio State," he said. "Coach Cooper called and offered me the opportunity of a lifetime, and I just couldn't pass it up."

Germaine is still remembered first for his heroics in the Rose Bowl, but that was just the beginning. Despite sharing quarterback duties with Jackson, he tossed for 1,847 yards in 1997, including 378 in relief against Penn State.

The next season, with the job all to himself, Germaine recorded seven 300-yard passing games, tossed twenty-five TDs, and broke the single-season school record with 3,330 yards. In his final game in Ohio Stadium, he torched Michigan for 330 yards passing and three touchdown tosses in a 31–16 walkover.

After setting eleven school records and leading OSU to another Big Ten title, Germaine won the prestigious Silver Football as the conference's MVP. With "Joe Cool" under center the Buckeyes held the number one ranking for ten straight weeks, which also tied a school mark.

Throughout his playing career and especially at Ohio State, Germaine not only had the cool to lead a team on drives and find receivers under pressure, he also had the toughness to take the hit. Former Ohio State offensive lineman Rob Murphy admitted having doubts that the 6', 200-pound Germaine would be able to take a hit until a rollout play in which the QB zipped right by him looking for a few yards.

"We have a verbal cue for that but he never said anything," Murphy said in 1998, "so I'm standing there blocking nobody. He made me look like an ass on national TV.

"I went up to him in the huddle and said, 'Joe, you've got to tell me when you're doing that. I'll at least try to get in somebody's way for you.'

"But how can you really be mad at a guy like that? He's a tough nut."

Just like a buckeye.

not start Stanley Jackson when we were 10–0 . . . no matter how good the other guy is doing you don't change."

Germaine was jittery early—he overshot an open Stanley in the end zone on one play—but he staked OSU to a 9–0 lead at halftime on three drives that led to short Josh Jackson field goals.

Then, the real omen came. On the second play from scrimmage of the second half, Springs slipped defending UM's Tai Streets, reserve quarterback Brian Griese hit him in stride, and Streets ran untouched for a 69-yard touchdown, the longest play of the season for Michigan and the most alarming of the year for the Buckeyes.

OSU had to dominate the first half to build up a lead. It was trimmed to almost nothing on one fluke play. "It was like we were losing even though we weren't," wide receiver Dee Miller said. "You could feel some guys tighten up."

Michigan didn't actually take the lead until the last play of the third quarter on a Remy Hamilton field goal. He added another with 1:19 to go and Germaine was unable to mount a rally despite pleas from a distressed record crowd.

Germaine, who completed just twelve of thirty-one passes, placed blame on himself afterward. Jackson threw just four passes in his short time on the field, completing one. Ironically, in the game Germaine and Jackson became the first OSU duo to surpass 1,000 yards passing in the same season. But that stat didn't begin to stave off second-guessers—or help anyone swallow yet another painful defeat at the hands of OSU's most bitter rival.

"It's an awful feeling," fullback Matt Calhoun said after the game. "I had hoped I would never have to feel it again and here I am, feeling it again."

Plenty happened in the weeks between the Michigan mess and the upcoming bowl game, but none of it seemed to alleviate any of the sting. Days after the game, postseason plaudits still rolled in for Buckeyes. Meanwhile, valuable offensive assistants Joe Hollis and Walt Harris, who were credited for the imagination of the offense, found head coaching jobs. Hollis, Cooper's offensive coordinator, took an offer to become the head coach and AD at Arkansas State. Harris, OSU's well-regarded quarterbacks coach, was announced as the new boss at Pittsburgh, a team OSU had bombed that season.

Those two stayed on for the sake of the Rose Bowl effort, but tackles and tight ends coach Mike Jacobs would take over play-calling duties, something he did for nine years at West Virginia under Don Nehlen.

"It was good that they stayed on for the continuity of the staff and at game time they were involved like always," Jacobs said of Hollis and Harris. "But let's face it, they were not using all their time to prepare for Arizona State. Those guys were busy putting together their staffs and getting ready to be head coaches."

The Makeup

All signs were pointing to disaster for the Buckeyes. Fans were still bitter about the team again losing its grip on a shot at the national championship. The quarterback saga was dissected by the media for weeks. Cooper's bowl record (1–6) was rearing its ugly head. Pac-10 champ Arizona State was talking about a national championship.

Despite it all, the Buckeyes had a sense of destiny in California and were able to focus enough to produce one of the most thrilling wins in program history.

The Pancake Man

After the 1996 regular season, several members of the vaunted Ohio State defense claimed awards.

Defensive end Mike Vrabel and cornerback Shawn Springs were named to several All-America teams. Linebacker Andy Katzenmoyer joined them on the All–Big Ten first team and was named the conference's Freshman of the Year. Defensive end Matt Finkes was named first-team All–Big Ten by the league coaches.

Even linebacker Greg Bellisari was recognized as an Academic All-American as well as a National Football Foundation and NCAA Post-Graduate Scholarship winner.

The offense had but one standout player, but did he ever make up for the others. Orlando Pace, a 6'6", 320-pound combination of brute strength and amazing athletic grace, proved in his junior season just how much of a factor a dominating trenchman can be to a team bucking for a national championship.

In fact Pace may have had the best season ever for an offensive lineman in college. At left tackle he stonewalled pass rushers and bought the scrambling Stanley Jackson and the ever-patient Joe Germaine valuable extra seconds. He blew open holes with regularity for tailback Pepe Pearson, who rushed for nearly 1,500 yards. He graded out between 85 and 94 percent all season.

"You cannot have a finer offensive lineman playing for you than Orlando Pace," said his OSU head coach, John Cooper. "Every week for him was a clinic."

When Pace was seen blocking some 50 yards downfield in the 1996 season opener and obliterating some of the best defensive ends in the country, some wondered if he could actually contend for the Heisman Trophy. OSU didn't lobby him as such but printed out statistics of pancakes—blocks that leave defenders laying flat on the turf—and handed out magnets of a stack of pancakes with Pace's name on them to the media.

Pace amassed eighty pancakes in 1996. Not since the 1970s, when Bill Fralic of Pitt and Ohio State's John Hicks (who actually was the 1973 Heisman runner-up), could anyone remember someone so dominating at offensive tackle.

The Big Ten coaches picked Pace as the unanimous Offensive Lineman of the Year and Player of the Year, and Pace won the *Chicago Tribune* Silver Football Award as conference MVP and the Outland Trophy as the nation's top interior lineman, and claimed the Lombardi Award for the second straight year, becoming the first two-time winner of the hardware.

Pace, who would go on to be taken with the first overall pick of the 1997 NFL draft by the St. Louis Rams, also finished fourth in the Heisman Trophy balloting. But he said that never motivated him.

"I just want to be the best college lineman ever," he said during the 1996 season. "I think I'm on pace."

"Obviously, when I think of that Rose Bowl I've got a lot of good memories," Cooper said from his central Ohio home six years later. "But probably as much as anything I remember them taking the lead. Jake Plummer made a great, great play and I remember looking across the field at them celebrating on their sideline.

"I remember all that in my mind because of the way we came back."

The game was a dogfight from the start. OSU drew first blood when Stanley Jackson, who drew the start, rolled right and found Boston for a 9-yard scoring strike. Arizona State tied the game as Plummer answered on a questionable 25-yard TD pass that appeared to slip through Ricky Boyer's hands and hit the ground. ASU added a field goal early in the third quarter to grab a 10–7 lead.

That's when Dimitrious Stanley made his mark. The OSU flanker noticed the ASU defense was aligned to give the wideouts the middle of the field and finally made the Sun Devils pay with a grab of a Germaine lob and a 72-yard TD that sent the OSU faithful into a frenzy.

"I told them the whole first half to throw the ball to me across the middle of the field and 'I'll promise I'll score.' When Coach Harris came down at halftime I told him the same thing," he said.

"The first play of that drive, Joe hit me on a dig route. The next play they listened."

As Stanley crossed the goal line he heard goosebump-inducing roars of approval. He also remembered another promise he had given the day before. "We were on the field for the walk-through and I happened to be in the end zone that said 'Ohio State' with Matt Finkes," he recalled, "and I pointed to a spot next to where we were standing and I said,

'I'm going to score right here tomorrow.' That very spot is where I scored."

The Buckeyes looked like they were going to make the score stand up until Plummer got his team moving late in the game. He got a hot hand and set up first and goal with a clutch 29-yard completion on fourth and 4.

On third and goal from the 11, "The Snake" avoided a blitzing Katzenmoyer and slithered his way through the defense for the biggest touchdown of his life. It looked like the gods were frowning on OSU again as they trailed 17–14.

I had worked my way down to the sideline from the press box to see the last few minutes of the game. I was in prime viewing position when Plummer fell into the end zone and could well imagine the pit in the stomachs of all the OSU fans in the stands and no doubt the ones standing in front of their couches at home.

I was beginning to have thoughts of having to do interviews and stories after another heartbreaking defeat. "What am I even going to ask these guys after this?" I thought as I turned toward Channel 10 sports anchor Mike Gleason, one of the most pleasant people in the business.

"A minute-forty," Gleason said. "A lot of time."

It suddenly dawned on me that he was right. After all, ASU had struggled to stop OSU's receivers whenever the Buckeyes tried to go down field. Cooper said he had the same feeling on the sideline. "I just thought that situation was tailor-made for Joe," he said. "He's probably the most poised football player you could ever hope to coach. Actually, I had a very confident feeling on the sideline."

Arizona State played it safe by kicking off short to upback Matt Keller, but they didn't expect the fullback to be so agile. He gave OSU excellent field position by zipping up to the 35 yard line. Then OSU put together one of its most memorable drives, as calm number 7 led the way.

"You could just look into Joe's eyes and see the determination," Pace said.

Germaine converted two third-and-10 situations with clutch strikes, both of them to Stanley. He dialed up Stanley again, moving the Buckeyes to the ASU 29 with forty-six seconds left.

OSU was within field-goal range but wasn't thinking about a tie, especially after the Devils committed a couple obvious defensive pass interference penalties. On first and goal from the ASU 5, Germaine again dropped back, looked off Stanley on a slant route, and flipped a pass out in the flat to Boston. The frosh caught the soft aerial at the 2 and turned and strolled into the end zone untouched with nineteen seconds left. The Buckeye Nation went crazy.

Jacobs, who had called "240 Smash" from the press box, also erupted with joy.

"Walt and I hugged each other to death," he said.

"Joe Germaine was like a surgeon going down that field," Cooper said. "And we got a great mismatch on that last drive. That guy had no chance trying to cover David Boston. He looked like a spastic to be honest with you. It was like shooting fish in a barrel."

It turned out the touchdown was an easier play for the Buckeyes than the extra point. In the chaos following the go-ahead score, Cooper called a time-out to make certain the best plan was to kick the extra point. Of course it was since OSU led by three. But Josh Jackson's low attempt was blocked.

Arizona State head coach Bruce Snyder said afterward that his team didn't lose the game, they just ran out of time. He may have been right. Plummer looked like he had a little

David Boston glides into the end zone with the game-winning TD after juk-ing an overmatched Arizona State defender. The last-minute score ruined the Sun Devils' bid for the national title. (Brockway Sports Photos)

magic left in him, completing a pass down to the OSU 35. But when the clock read :00 and the scoreboard 20–17, his great college career had ended a few points short of a national title.

As pandemonium erupted on the field I happened to race through the crowd and right by Cooper, who turned to who-ever was within earshot and blurted, "Who says we can't win the big game?"

Meanwhile, the usually composed Andy Geiger was over-flowing with emotion. "We had to do the hard thing the hard way and did it," he said, voice cracking. "I think it's a real breakthrough for all of us."

A reporter then noted Geiger was crying.

"Yes I am," he said unashamedly. "We work hard at this. This is my life. I'm just so happy for these kids."

Clutch performances came from every direction. Jackson helped get things started with a TD toss in the first half, while Germaine pulled it out at the end. Stanley finished with five catches for 124 yards and the longest pass reception ever by a Buckeye in a bowl game.

Pearson logged his tenth 100-yard rushing output in the twelve-game season. His 1,484 yards were slightly better than the 1,450 of Archie Griffin's Heisman-winning season of 1975. Of course Pace, who was stellar all season, had a hand in that.

Boston had two touchdowns. Fellow frosh Katzenmoyer registered eight tackles, five of them in the backfield. "Andy Katzenmoyer—wow. That's all I can say," said Moore.

Moore was impressive as well with a dozen tackles, which gave him seasonal honors by one over Bellisari. The OSU captain also came up big in Pasadena with nine tackles. Also a standout on defense, Springs shut down ASU leading receiver Keith Poole, holding him to just one catch for 10 yards.

In short the defensive effort was superb. ASU came in averaging 492 yards and forty-two points per game. Those numbers were shaved to 276 and seventeen by the Buckeyes.

In their celebration on the field, the players said they would root for Florida to knock off unbeaten Florida State in the Sugar Bowl. However, they didn't count on Florida winning the rematch 52–20 or the game being billed as the national championship.

OSU, which had outscored foes by an average score of 38–11 on the season, got a handful of first-place votes but had to settle for second in both major polls. An 11–1 record that included a 3–0 mark against top-five teams just wasn't good enough.

The BCS would come up with a new system for determining a number one versus number two matchup just two years later, something Cooper had stumped for even before the 1996 season. "I know people now can't stop talking about the [2003] Fiesta Bowl," Cooper said. "But to me, to beat a team that was going to be undisputed national champion and to come back the way we did—in the Rose Bowl—that's as good as it gets."

Never a Dull Moment Covering the Buckeyes

L et's just say that coverage of Ohio State football, especially in the electronic media, has evolved a bit.

In the 1960s and 1970s about the only extra analysis concerning games would come via *The Woody Hayes Show* on television, in which the well-respected OSU coach would touch on highlights of that weekend's game, delve into his Pattonlike philosophies, and even invite members of his team to explain what transpired.

Particularly hard to watch was the players standing like wooden soldiers and droning answers like "Yes, sir," "No, sir," and "We'll have to do better on that play next time, Coach." Still, they participated without complaint.

"You know why we all loved doing that show?" said former Buckeye Larry Zelina (1968–70). "The old man would reach into his wallet and give us each $5.00 for being on it. Hey, back then to have some extra money and be able to go get a couple double cheeseburgers was a big deal. We were happier than a pet raccoon."

Woody actually taught his own class while at Ohio State. It helped new students learn the layout of campus, how to schedule classes, proper etiquette and grammar, and so on. Today, student-athletes actually get a couple of PE credits for a media training course, which of course, teaches them to answer questions as if they were androids—just like Woody did.

However, the scope of media coverage has changed drastically in the last couple decades. In Columbus several different radio stations—such as WTVN-AM (610) and WBNS-AM (1460)—and all the local television stations fill their airwaves with Buckeyes chatter. Newspaper beat writers come from every nook and cranny of the state for games and the team's weekly media luncheon. The *Columbus Dispatch* unashamedly has as many as eight reporters and a half-dozen photographers at games. In-depth fan publication *Buckeye Sports Bulletin* has grown yearly in its circulation and, among other things, pounds football recruiting.

And the national coverage is thick: *USA Today*, *Sports Illustrated*, *The Sporting News*, *ESPN: The Magazine*, and just about every other formidable publication is sniffing around the program on a very regular basis. Web sites also get in the act. Buckeye highlights—with scrolls of scores and team news below—are regular features on ESPN, Fox Sports Net, and CNN, among others.

A new Ohio Stadium press box was built at the turn of the millennium to accommodate hundreds of reporters for game day, and the sports information office still has to turn some applicants away.

It's sometimes difficult to have an intimate working relationship with all the hoopla going on—even secure practices are littered with "friends of the program"—but there are those rare opportunities when you get excellent feature quotes from a one-on-one interview or are one of just a few posing questions to a coach or player. Plus, everyone has his own unique experiences.

Checking Your Allegiance at the Door

When most people hear you are a sportswriter and that you get to go to all of the Ohio State football games, they immediately become jealous at the thought of someone getting to watch football from a free seat in the press box and then getting to talk to coaches and players afterward. Well, it's not always that much fun or that simple, especially for the reporters who are on tight deadlines.

Rusty Miller of the Associated Press in Columbus had twenty-three years of covering the Buckeyes under his belt when he headed to the 2003 Fiesta Bowl. It turned out all the excitement on the field was just a sideshow for what was going on at Rusty's perch atop the Sun Devil Stadium press box.

He checked in with the AP office in New York City midway through the third quarter and confirmed he could send them a story on OSU quarterback Craig Krenzel to be run nationally. The editor at the New York desk then put the pressure on, telling Miller, "And we need it within one minute after the game ends."

As Miami (Florida) was driving in the final minute, Miller read his story one last time and readied to send it. Then, mysteriously, his screen blipped out. He described the emotional roller coaster he was on while everyone else was wrapped up in what was billed as the most exciting national championship game ever.

"As I got to the penultimate paragraph . . . my screen went blank," he said. "The story was gone, a vapor. Knowing it wouldn't do any good, I nonetheless tried several things to see if I could somehow revive the lost words. Nothing.

"Just then, Miami came out of a time-out to try the tying field goal. The crowd was frenzied. All around me, writers were furiously typing away to complete stories.

"Me? After more than two decades of covering Ohio State football, I found myself standing, not saying a thing but screaming inside for Miami to *kick the field goal so I could come up with another story!*

"When the kick sailed through the uprights, millions of Ohio State fans across the country sank back into their seats in disappointment that the game wasn't over, that it would be going to overtime. And here I was, smugly smiling to myself because I had bought enough time that I now could re-create the lost story."

Miller did just that. He banged out 600 words and sent it in within a minute of OSU's 31–24 double-overtime victory. It ran to just about every sports department in every newspaper, television station, and radio station in America.

"In retrospect, the story behind the story was probably more interesting than what I attached my name to," he said.

But that's the goal—get the story out no matter what.

Former Buckeye Raymont Harris was on the Ohio State sideline cheering on his team because he was not given an assignment by WBNS, a radio station that touts itself—along with dozens of others—as "The Fan."

"I went in the locker room after the game with the other guys [former players] and we were all celebrating and jumping around," said the former running back, who is sometimes critical of the team but never hides the fact he still wants the Buckeyes to win.

That's when 350-pound offensive lineman Adrien Clarke sought out Harris, who had talked about Clarke's weight on the air earlier that season.

"He came up to me and said, 'Yeah, you thought I was too fat, huh?' I thought, 'Oh damn, I am one of the media now.' I still think of myself as one of the guys but I need to remember they don't all see me that way."

Marvelous Marv

Reporters are hesitant to admit it, but there is a small group of people out there who make them look knowledgeable—sports information staff. After all, they are the ones that feed press releases, statistics, schedules, television info, and sometimes quotes to reporters. They also oversee coordination of all interview sessions and press conferences.

Somehow, Marv Homan managed to do all that and remain one of the most likable guys in the business. "He was always a great guy to deal with. Very pleasant and a very classy guy. He simply wouldn't say anything bad about anybody," said George Strode, who covered Ohio State football for the Associated Press and served as sports editor of the *Columbus Dispatch.*

"Sometimes it'd be tough because if you approached him about something controversial, he'd say, 'Frankly, George, I simply don't know,' which may have been true. Today, the sports information people are more intimately involved and it seems like they're part of the cover-up more than getting the reporters the information.

"Marv was the opposite. He had no interest in getting involved in the dirty work. He just wanted to get you the information."

Homan was an assistant sports information director at Ohio State from 1949 to 1972 and served as SID from 1973 until the end of the 1987 when he retired. It was a profession he never intended to enter.

A native of Dayton, Homan graduated from Ohio State in 1948. During his junior and senior years, he worked at the school radio station, WOSU, and conducted a nightly sports show. Homan eventually landed a gig as the color commentator for the OSU football broadcasts and figured he could keep his toe in that pool by accepting a job with sports information, under SID Wilbur Snypp.

"I learned a lot from him," he said. "He was a newspaper man so he knew that point of view and I picked up on the radio aspect from my background."

But the job proved to be much more than providing for those two mediums. The football team's popularity exploded in the 1950s with the arrival of Woody Hayes and national championships in 1954 and 1957. Newspapers from all over the state were descending on Ohio Stadium and national magazines such as *Sports Illustrated* came into being. Plus, television coverage was growing exponentially.

While keeping up with all that with a very limited staff, Homan also spent thirty years (1950–79) as the football play-by-play man for the radio network. In his first year at the mike for football, Homan called the infamous Snow Bowl of 1950. OSU lost the game with Michigan 9–3 in a blizzard, the only Buckeye points coming on a miraculous 38-yard field goal by Heisman Trophy winner Vic Janowicz.

"I could vaguely make out the official's signal that it was good, but I didn't see the ball in flight and I didn't see it come down," Homan said. "That game was absolutely unlike any game I ever did in thirty years of play-by-play broadcasting and unlike anything I have ever seen."

Near the end of Homan's tenure as SID, Hayes was fired directly after the 1978 Gator Bowl for punching a Clemson player. "That was the most difficult situation I ever had to deal with," Homan said. "It was difficult for two reasons: one, to have a great career go out in such an inglorious manner, and two, that was just a logistical nightmare in Jacksonville. There was an impromptu press conference the next morning at the team hotel, which was not set up for that sort of thing. The hotel was on the Jacksonville beach and hard to find. I didn't know where a lot of people were staying. Some left that night. That was just no fun."

But Homan, as always, never grumbled and did the best he could. It was that very kind of effort—as well as his longstanding service to the university—that earned him recognition in the OSU Athletics Hall of Fame. "I really regarded that as a great honor," Homan said.

Matthew Bretscher of WTVN has gathered quotes and done radio reports with his smooth voice and quick wit for years. Anyone would tell you Matt, a former OSU swim captain, is one of the nicest guys in the business. But being on the front lines — that is, interviewing coaches and players, sometimes in trying times — has still caused some to be testy with him.

Bretscher remembers vividly the bad vibe in the air November 5, 1998, just two days before a very fateful Saturday in Columbus. As was the weekly norm, he was on hand for Thursday interviews with head coach John Cooper. Bretscher was told by the sports information attendant on hand that interviews would proceed as normal: electronic media first and then print media. Cooper, for whatever reason, wanted to do just TV first and waved in the local cameramen.

When Bretscher leaned in with his radio microphone unaware of the change, Cooper shoved him aside, knocking him off balance and yelled, "What are you doing in here. I'll get to you later."

"I talked to a couple reporters afterward and they all agreed that Coop was getting tight, which, to me, wasn't a good sign," Bretscher said. "I remember I went home and told my wife, 'I think Ohio State's in trouble.' "

That Saturday, the top-ranked Buckeyes hosted Michigan State. They were a four-touchdown favorite. OSU opened up a 24–9 lead and seemed to be in control. "I thought, 'I guess I was wrong,' " Bretscher said. But Michigan State roared back and posted a 28–24 upset that devastated OSU's national championship dreams.

The moral? Save the pushing around for the field.

Jimmy Crum can attest. Crum was the sports director at the NBC-affiliated local television station WCMH (previously WLWC) from 1951–93. In that time he was known for his nightly reports, wacky-patterned blazers, and insight into the local sports scene. He also was a tireless worker for charitable causes in the community.

And even though he graduated from Ohio University, Crum was deeply tied to Ohio State. He was a play-by-play broadcaster for the men's basketball team in the Fred Taylor glory days and was a clear supporter of Ohio State football. Nevertheless, when things weren't going well on the gridiron, Crum wasn't afraid to lash out with a biting commentary, even calling for Cooper's head in one veiny-necked episode.

As for dealing with Hayes, Crum worked with him without incident for years. But in 1965 Crum noticed Hayes was in a particularly foul mood as OSU hosted Minnesota for Homecoming.

Crum was down on the sideline noting plays for his evening highlights and was standing next to a freshman photographer for the *Lantern*, the school newspaper. The student was snapping picture after picture of Hayes blowing up on the sideline. Throwing down his hat and stomping on it were Hayes's favorite forms of disgust. On this day Hayes even decided to stomp on his own glasses.

When walking off the field at halftime, Woody approached the student and said, "You shoot one more f_ing picture of me with that f_ing camera and I'm going to shove that f_ing camera up your f_ing ass."

OSU won 11–10 on a last-second field goal but Hayes was still unsatisfied with the performance. Still, Crum confronted Hayes after the game and told him he had no right to stop reporters from doing their jobs.

"It's my goddam stadium and I'll do anything I want in it," Hayes told him.

"I said, 'Well I think you're horses_t and bush league' and he started after me," Crum recalled. "Dick Otte [another

The One and Only Woody

Wayne Woodrow Hayes was a lot of things to a lot of people, but to the media he was both an absolute gem and a royal pain in the derriere. Despite his often gruff demeanor and insistence on doing things the safe and moral way, Hayes was a character. He wasn't afraid to say anything to anybody, and he had either a trite opinion or a well-deep theorem on just about every topic imaginable. And Hayes was even accessible. In fact his home phone number was listed throughout his coaching days.

In his twenty-eight years at the helm he certainly turned off his share of writers. Longtime *Sports Illustrated* football writer Paul Zimmerman once said of Hayes, "If I were a young player I'd give my left testicle to play for him. But I also know his general opinion of the press, and as a sportswriter you couldn't pay me enough to cover him on a regular basis."

Those on the beat quickly found out what was printable in Hayes's eyes and what was off-limits. One day, longtime WCMH-TV sports director Jimmy Crum went to see Hayes in the coach's north facility office, which is now known as the Ernie Biggs facility (and appropriately is a wing in the current Woody Hayes Athletic Center).

"I noticed he had an erector set in his office and I said, 'Hey, Coach, are you in your second childhood?' " Crum said. "He explained it wasn't his, that it was for a sick kid at University Hospital, and that he had planned to take it over to him after practice. And then he leaned over his desk and looked at me and said, 'If you say one goddamn word about this I'll kick you right in the ass.'

"Woody liked to keep his reputation as a hard guy and didn't want people to know all the good deeds."

After he was fired for punching Clemson's Charlie Bauman, Hayes eventually sought out the youngster and spent an entire day with him. No one in the media found out for years.

Hayes was always good copy. He fired off an uncountable number of zingers, many of them coming away from the football field. Hayes was known for pulling a student aside on the campus Oval or greeting folks at his favorite restaurant and always being ready with a word of advice.

Many in Columbus still mention Hayes talking about "paying forward." Another slogan directly associated with Hayes—"You win with people."—is visible in the atrium of the football team's training complex.

Those who knew Hayes said he was stubborn enough to insist that what he thought was right, no matter how wrong it was. But it usually wasn't wrong when it came to football as a mark of 205–61–10 at OSU attests. And when Hayes spoke, truth and witticism usually spilled out.

For example, Hayes once told reporters, "If people don't criticize Woody Hayes, there's something wrong with them. I walked by the mirror Sunday and almost took a swing at him." He also was quoted as saying, "The Bible says turn the other cheek, but I'll be damned if I'll tell my kids to do that when they'll just get it fractured."

In his time on campus after his firing, Hayes's legend only grew. In his first public appearance after his shameful exit, Hayes received a standing ovation. He maintained an office at the ROTC building and coaches of other programs often brought recruits by to see Woody, which often sealed the deal.

The late Woody Hayes became even more well known—and sometimes more endeared—for his famous tirades.
(Brockway Sports Photos)

Even after Hayes's passing in 1987 many still tried to figure him out and put into words what he meant to those he left behind. Archie Griffin may have found the simple answer when he said, "Woody is a God-fearing man. It's nice to know he's afraid of somebody."

reporter] got in between us or there would have been blood shed—probably mine."

Hayes did not utter a word directly at Crum for six months after that, but opportunity knocked one day when Crum entered an old diner on Olentangy River Road, just down the street from the station and also very close to campus. When he walked in he noticed Hayes alone.

Crum asked to sit down.

"How ya doing, Jim. I've hardly seen you," said the coach.

Crum then told Hayes he assumed Hayes hated him.

"I still don't agree with what you said but, goddammit, I give you credit for having the guts to say it," said the coach.

Crum hosted a local Easter Seals telethon for twenty-two straight years and Hayes graciously appeared every year for about an hour or so. Before Hayes headed out, Crum would always make a point to thank the tireless coach and shake his hand. Hayes would shake firmly back and leave a wadded up piece of paper in Crum's right hand.

"It was always a $50 or $20 bill," he said.

Hayes also participated in Celebrity Waiters and Recreation Unlimited charity functions with Crum.

When Earle Bruce was hired in 1979, Crum also developed a rapport with the former OSU assistant. It didn't hurt that Bruce used to be a high school coach in Mansfield, Crum's hometown.

"One of the nicest guys I've ever met," Crum said. "But he was feisty, too. I asked him once in private, 'Is there a little Woody in you?' And Earle replied, 'I sure as hell hope so.' "

The two hit it off so well that when Bruce's contract for his television show on WBNS (Channel 10) expired he negotiated his own deal with WCMH to be with Crum, who hosted the show in 1985 and 1986. "That irked John W. Wolfe (owner of

WBNS and the *Columbus Dispatch*) to no end," Crum said.

The inside word is that Wolfe made pleas to the board of trustees and university president Ed Jennings to fire Bruce. They got their chance when the Buckeyes slipped to 6–4–1 in 1987. Bruce was gone. Before leaving, though, he offered Crum a token of his appreciation—his 1986 Big Ten championship ring.

Crum had no such connection with Bruce's replacement, John Cooper. In fact Crum broadcast scathing commentaries after Cooper's Buckeyes lost to Air Force in the 1990 Liberty Bowl and to Illinois in 1992.

"We didn't get along too well," said Crum, who retired in 1993 and now resides in Dublin, Ohio.

Beat Writers Strode, Kessler Saw It All

George Strode's powerful position in the media had its advantages and its downside, like drawing the ire of the head coach.

As the sports editor of the *Columbus Dispatch*, Strode got inside word—and printed it—that Cooper was going to be canned if the Buckeyes lost a fifth straight game to archrival Michigan in 1992. When OSU managed a 13–13 tie, Cooper approached Strode in a packed postgame interview room and blasted him with sarcasm.

"Really appreciate your coverage this week, George," he said.

"We had that from a very good source," Strode said. "It was going to happen. But I don't think anyone had a plan in mind for a tie.

Many years later Strode said: "I truly believe that's why [former university president] Gordon Gee said it was the greatest victory ever."

Strode had a little more perspective on the matter than Gee, Cooper, and just about everyone else. He had been a sportswriter for the now-defunct Columbus *Citizen-Journal* from 1963 to 1969, left to take over duties as the Ohio sports editor for the Associated Press from 1969 to 1985 and enjoyed his reign as *Dispatch* sports editor from 1985–99 before retiring.

Another fixture of the Ohio Stadium press box was Kaye Kessler, a sportswriter for the *Citizen* from 1941 to 1959 and the *Citizen-Journal*, as it became known, from 1959 until the paper closed shop in December 1985. Kessler, an author who now resides in Denver and still writes for the *Denver Post*, also was a well-read columnist for the *C-J* in the 1970s and 1980s.

While covering all twenty-eight years of the Woody Hayes era (1951–78), Kessler had to compete with the *Dispatch's* Paul Hornung, who happened to be Hayes's close friend.

"Woody was a curmudgeon and Paul Hornung was his shadow, but it was fun back then and Woody and I always got along," Kessler said. "Frankly, I liked him very much."

Still, Kessler once got cornered by Hayes while out in California to cover the 1958 Rose Bowl.

"Here we're out at the Rose Bowl and Ohio State is about to win the national championship and Woody comes up to me in the media lounge and says, 'Goddamn you. You picked us to finish seventh.' I said, 'I did not,' and the next thing you know we're butting bellies.

"A guy from the Pasadena paper is in there and the next day there's a big headline, 'Hayes, OSU Writer in Press Room Scuffle.' But, hey, it was fun covering that guy."

"Nobody could match the color of Woody Hayes," said Strode. "You never knew what he was going to do from day to day."

Strode particularly enjoyed covering the Archie Griffin–led Buckeyes of the 1970s in the Rose Bowl. One year, it actually rained for days in Southern California on the team's arrival there. Hayes, who despised practicing indoors, arranged to take his team to East Los Angeles Junior College.

Hayes would not let unfamiliar and West Coast reporters attend his practices so this particular session was staged before only Strode, Kessler, Hornung, and a writer for the Cleveland *Plain Dealer*. Because the field at East Los Angeles JUCO was anything but refined, it resembled a quagmire after two full days of rain and with a Big Ten team rummaging around on it. This, of course, was no excuse to Hayes, so when his punter was having trouble with his footing and handling snaps, he snapped.

"Goddammit, get out of there," he told his kicker. "I'll show you how to do it."

Hayes, who was left-handed and apparently left-footed, ordered the ball deep snapped to him, took a half step to catch it, tried to drive a kick, and fell directly on his posterior in the mud.

"Put that in your f_ing newspapers," he said to the quartet of reporters.

"That's the hardest time I ever had trying not to laugh in my life," Strode recalled. "He fell right on his duff. But you didn't dare laugh out loud or you'd be sent out the gate."

Obviously, covering Hayes was a supreme challenge, and Hayes didn't exactly give preferential treatment to the regular beat writers, except, of course, his buddy Hornung.

"One time we were up at Michigan after a game Ohio State had lost, which, you can imagine, didn't sit well with Woody," Strode said. "He let Hornung in the locker room and talked and talked to him. Then he came out all honked off and talked to the rest of us for twenty-nine seconds. Kessler timed him. That'll test you to write a 400-word sidebar on that."

Of course, Hayes's most infamous outburst cost him his job. Kessler and Strode were among the stunned gaggle of reporters at the 1978 Gator Bowl.

With the game winding down and reporters not wanting to fight through the crowd to get to the locker room, several went down to the sideline for the final minutes, Strode among them. He saw the Charlie Bauman interception and saw Bauman return it like he was running right at the OSU bench, but he didn't see much of what followed—Hayes grabbing Bauman and punching him in the throat with his right hand.

Still, Strode got all the accounts he could and wrote up the game and the incident. It was a long night that was about to get longer. At about 2:00 A.M. when he was having a nightcap in the media room, Strode noticed Nancy Hindman, wife of school AD Hugh Hindman. She was crying.

"I knew something was up," Strode said.

But no official announcement had been made and Strode finally retired to his hotel bed with his wife at about 3:00 A.M. A few hours later, the phone rang. It was word from the AP.

"Woody's been fired," a co-worker told Strode.

"Oh, hell," Strode responded.

Strode pulled on a pair of pants and a sports shirt in the dark so as not to wake up his wife and headed down to the lobby. Sure enough, he found Hugh Hindman in the coffee shop, interviewed him—bare feet and all—and went back to his room to work on one of the biggest stories ever to hit central Ohio.

"When I got upstairs I told my wife, 'These pants don't have any pockets on them,' and she said, 'That's because they're mine,' " he said.

Oh, the dangers of being a reporter.

About the Author

Jeff Rapp knew at a young age, maybe even as a toddler living in Southern California, that he wanted to associate his livelihood with sports. During formative years in Columbus, Ohio, he set out toward that dream by writing for his high school and college newspapers and, at 19, working as a technician for ABC-TV at the Los Angeles Memorial Coliseum for the 1984 Summer Olympics. It was there he got to witness the pageantry and drama of athletic competition on the highest scale. Back in Columbus, Ohio State football and basketball also got into his blood. He graduated with a degree in journalism from OSU in 1988 and quickly earned a job covering the Buckeyes for a fan publication. In 1992, he came on full board at *Buckeye Sports Bulletin*, where he has served as Senior Writer ever since. Rapp has been a tireless beat writer for football and men's basketball for a dozen years and also has had works published in several national magazines. Among his highlights were covering the 1997 Rose Bowl, the 1999 Final Four, and, of course, the 2003 Fiesta Bowl in which Ohio State won the BCS Championship.